RED & GREEN QUILTS

14 Classic Quilts with Enduring Appeal

Martingale®
Create with Confidence

Red & Green Quilts: 14 Classic Quilts with Enduring Appeal
© 2020 by Martingale & Company®

Martingale®
19021 120th Ave. NE, Ste. 102
Bothell, WA 98011-9511 USA
ShopMartingale.com

Printed in Hong Kong
25 24 23 22 21 20   8 7 6 5 4 3 2 1

Library of Congress Cataloging-in-Publication Data
is available upon request.

ISBN: 978-1-68356-107-1

MISSION STATEMENT

We empower makers who use fabric and yarn
to make life more enjoyable.

CREDITS

PUBLISHER AND
CHIEF VISIONARY OFFICER
Jennifer Erbe Keltner

CONTENT DIRECTOR
Karen Costello Soltys

DESIGN MANAGER
Adrienne Smitke

MANAGING EDITOR
Tina Cook

COVER AND BOOK DESIGNER
Regina Girard

ACQUISITIONS AND
DEVELOPMENT EDITOR
Laurie Baker

PHOTOGRAPHERS
Brent Kane
Adam Albright

TECHNICAL WRITER
Elizabeth Beese

ILLUSTRATOR
Sandy Loi

TECHNICAL EDITOR
Ellen Pahl

COPY EDITOR
Sheila Chapman Ryan

SPECIAL THANKS

Photography for this book was taken at the homes of:
Karen Burns in Carnation, Washington
Tracie Fish in Kenmore, Washington
Bree Larson in Everett, Washington
Julie Smiley in Des Moines, Iowa

CONTENTS

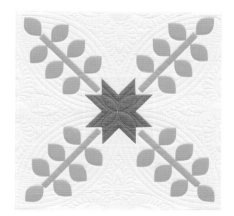

INTRODUCTION

Classic color combinations are favored by many quilters who long to create timeless quilts that can be enjoyed generation after generation. Firmly embedded in the ranks of "favorite duos," red-and-green is every bit the enduring pairing that blue-and-white and red-and-white have become.

In the late nineteenth century, young girls were taught the needle arts, and quiltmaking was an integral part of that training. During that same period, red-and-green appliqué quilts were quite prevalent. Interestingly, the two most common times in a woman's life when she would make a red-and-green quilt were just before (or immediately after) her marriage, and again when she reached forty or fifty years of age. The latter quilt, ostensibly, was made as her children were leaving home and she had more leisure time to pursue her own interests.

Times have changed, but the captivating appeal of red-and-green quilts has not, whether patchwork, appliqué, or a combination of the two. This compendium of two-color quilts (mostly, though some quiltmakers couldn't resist tossing in a little cheddar for dramatic effect) includes must-make quilt patterns by 15 of today's top designers. Each quilt imbues the lasting beauty you and your family will treasure for years to come. Why not get started on your next classic quilt today?

~Jennifer Erbe Keltner

THEODOR'S WORLD

BY LAURIE SIMPSON

I enjoyed making this whimsical quilt in reds and greens. When finished, it looked very Dr. Seuss–like to me, hence the name—an appreciative nod to Theodor Seuss Geisel, one of the most popular children's book authors of all time. ~Laurie

Materials

Yardage is based on 42"-wide fabric.

1⅝ yards *total* of assorted red prints for blocks, middle border, and berry appliqués

3⅛ yards of white solid for blocks and borders

¾ yard *total* of assorted green prints and solids for leaf appliqués

½ yard of olive green solid for binding

3⅓ yards of fabric for backing

59" × 59" piece of batting

Copy paper (18- or 20-lb rather than 24-lb) or foundation-piecing material of your choice

Olive green pearl cotton #12

Perfect Circles 1¼" and 1" heat-resistant templates by Karen Kay Buckley *or* heat-resistant template plastic for berries

Freezer paper or other template material for leaves

Spray starch or starch alternative

Bloc Loc Flying Geese Square Up Ruler, 1¼" × 2½" (optional)

Cutting

All measurements include ¼" seam allowances.

From the assorted red prints, cut:

25 strips, 1½" × 8¼" (piece 1)

50 strips, 1½" × 6½" (pieces 3 and 7)

25 squares, 3" × 3"; cut in half diagonally to make 50 triangles (pieces 5 and 9)

104 squares, 2¼" × 2¼"; cut in half diagonally to make 208 triangles

Save all remaining fabrics for appliqués.

From the *lengthwise* grain of the white solid, cut:

2 strips, 9" × 52½"

2 strips, 9" × 35½"

From the *remainder* of the white solid, cut:

3 strips, 4" × 42"; crosscut into 26 squares, 4" × 4". Cut into quarters diagonally to make 104 triangles.

4 strips, 3" × 42"; crosscut into:
  2 strips, 3" × 30½"
  2 strips, 3" × 25½"

17 strips, 1½" × 42"; crosscut into:
  50 strips, 1½" × 7½" (pieces 2 and 6)
  50 strips, 1½" × 5" (pieces 4 and 8)

From the olive green solid, cut:

6 strips, 2½" × 42"

By Laurie Simpson

Quilt Size: 52½" × 52½" **Block Size:** 5" × 5"

Making the Blocks

Press all seam allowances as indicated by the arrows.

1. Using your choice of foundation-piecing material, make 25 copies of the block foundation pattern on page 12. Cut out each copy roughly ¼" outside the dashed outer line.

2. Place a red print 1½" × 8¼" strip right side up on the wrong side of the foundation, covering space 1. Hold the paper up to the light to check positioning. Place a white solid 1½" × 7½" strip right sides together with the red strip, centering it over the red strip. Pin the strips in place from the paper side.

3. With the marked side of the paper facing up, sew on the line between spaces 1 and 2. Remove the unit from the machine and press the white strip over to cover space 2.

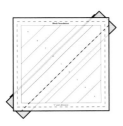

4. Working in numerical order, add red print and white solid strips and red 3" triangles for pieces 3–9 to cover the foundation paper. Trim on the dashed line to make a block that's 5½" square, including seam allowances. Repeat to make 25 blocks.

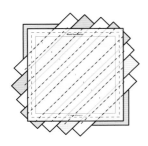
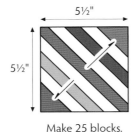

Make 25 blocks.

Assembling the Quilt Center

1. Lay out the blocks in five rows of five blocks each, rotating the blocks as shown in the quilt assembly diagram below.

2. Sew the blocks together in each row, and then join the rows. Remove the foundation papers. The quilt center should measure 25½" square, including seam allowances.

Quilt assembly

Making the Pieced Borders

1. Sew red 2¼" triangles to both short edges of a white 4" triangle as shown to make a flying-geese unit. Using the Bloc Loc Flying Geese Square Up Ruler or an acrylic ruler, trim the unit to 1¾" × 3", including seam allowances. Make 104 flying-geese units.

Make 104 units.

2. Sew together 24 flying-geese units as shown to make a middle-border strip that measures 3" × 30½", including seam allowances. Make two for the sides of the quilt center.

Make 2 borders, 3" × 30½".

3. Sew together 28 flying-geese units, rotating two units as shown, to make a middle-border strip that measures 3" × 35½", including seam allowances. Make two for the top and bottom.

Make 2 borders, 3" × 35½".

Making the Appliquéd Borders

For more information on appliqué techniques, go to ShopMartingale.com/HowtoQuilt.

1. *If not using Perfect Circles,* make templates by tracing the large and small berry patterns on page 13 once onto heat-resistant template plastic. Cut out smoothly on the drawn lines. Make templates for the leaves using freezer paper or your preferred template material.

2. Cut out 16 assorted green leaves, 32 assorted large red berries, and 64 assorted small red berries, adding ¼" seam allowances all around each piece.

3. Hand- or machine-sew a basting stitch within the seam allowance of each red circle. Center the 1¼" Perfect Circle (or large berry template) on the wrong side of a large red circle. Gather the basting stitches tightly around the template, then apply starch and press until dry. Allow to cool and then remove the stitches and template. Repeat to prepare each large berry appliqué. Repeat with the 1" Perfect Circle (or small berry template) and small red circles.

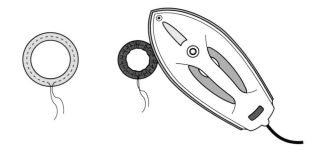

4. Prepare the leaves using your preferred appliqué method.

5. Referring to the diagrams below and the photo on page 8, measure and mark the placement for each section of appliqué on the white 9"-wide strips. In each 9⅜"-wide section of the strip, position and appliqué one leaf, two large berries, and four small berries.

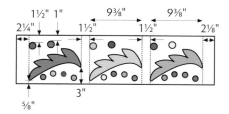

Make 2 appliquéd borders, 9" × 35½".

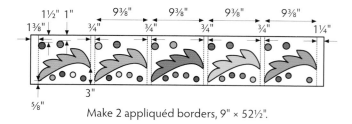

Make 2 appliquéd borders, 9" × 52½".

6. Lightly mark a stem if desired, and stitch a line connecting each berry appliqué to the leaf appliqué. Stem-stitch using olive green pearl cotton.

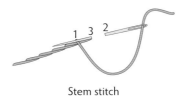

Stem stitch

Adding the Borders

1. Sew the white 3" × 25½" strips to opposite sides of the quilt center. Add the white 3" × 30½" strips to the top and bottom. The quilt center should now be 30½" square, including seam allowances.

2. Sew the shorter flying-geese border strips to opposite sides of the quilt center, paying attention to the direction of the flying geese. In the same manner, sew the longer border strips to the top and bottom. The quilt center should now be 35½" square, including seam allowances.

3. Sew the shorter appliquéd borders to opposite sides of the quilt center. Add the longer appliquéd borders to the top and bottom to complete the quilt top, which should measure 52½" square.

Adding the borders

Finishing the Quilt

For more details on any finishing steps, visit ShopMartingale.com/HowtoQuilt for free downloadable information.

1. Layer the backing, batting, and quilt top; baste the layers together.

2. Quilt by hand or machine. The quilt shown is hand quilted through the center of each strip and triangle in the pieced blocks and with a leaf design in the inner border. In the middle border, each white triangle is outline quilted ¼" from the edges, and there is a line of quilting through the center of each red triangle. The appliquéd border is quilted with a diagonal crosshatch in the background. Each appliqué is outline quilted, and each leaf has a line of quilting inside, approximately ¼" from the edge.

3. Use the olive green solid 2½"-wide strips to make binding, and then attach the binding to the quilt.

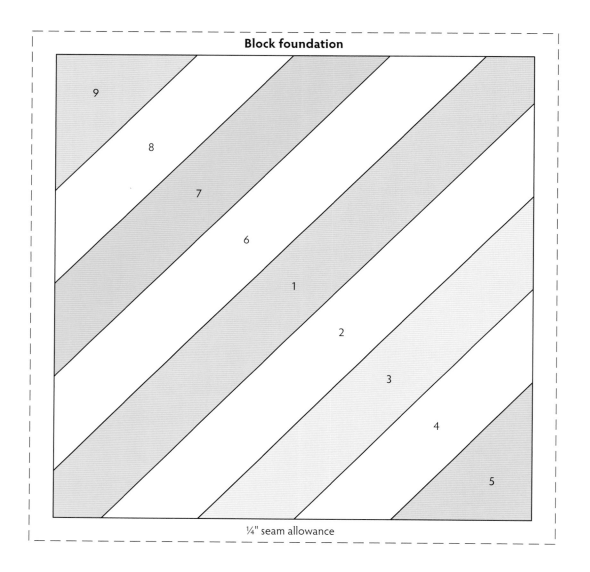

Block foundation

¼" seam allowance

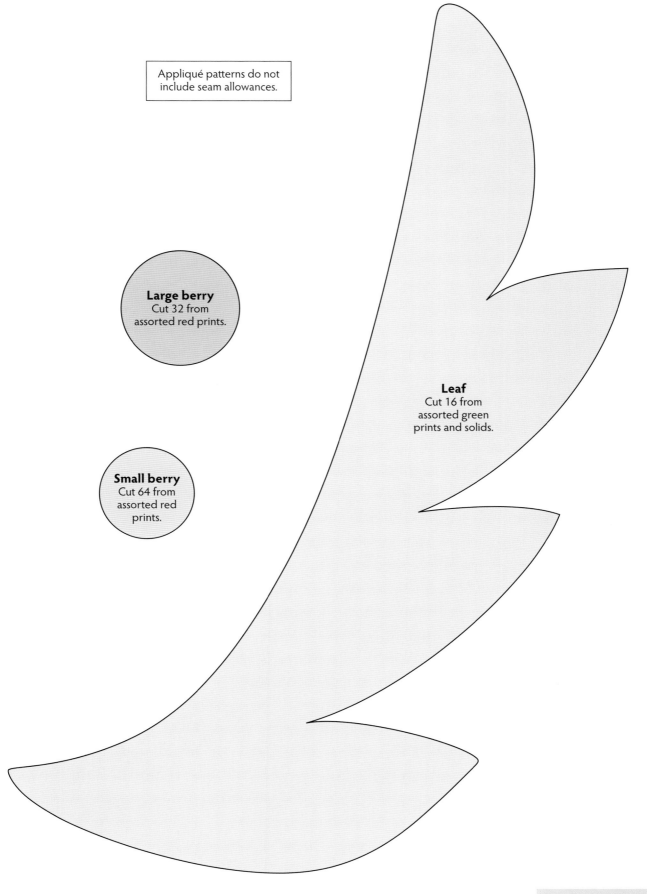

Appliqué patterns do not include seam allowances.

Large berry
Cut 32 from assorted red prints.

Leaf
Cut 16 from assorted green prints and solids.

Small berry
Cut 64 from assorted red prints.

STARSTRUCK

BY SUSAN ACHE

Have you heard it said that "All greens go together"? I believe it's true in quilts as well as in nature. While I've leaned heavily on yellow-greens for my quilt, you can safely go with a wider variety of greens if you prefer. It will be awesome no matter what! ~Susan

Materials

Yardage is based on 42"-wide fabric. Fat quarters measure 18" × 21".

29 strips, 2" × 21", of assorted red prints for blocks

29 strips, 2" × 21", of assorted white-with-red prints for blocks

18 fat quarters of assorted white-with-green prints for blocks and outer border

18 fat quarters of assorted green prints for blocks and borders

¾ yard of white floral for sashing and inner border

1 yard of red floral for sashing

¼ yard of red diagonal check for sashing squares*

⅔ yard of green floral for binding

7 yards of fabric for backing

83" × 83" piece of batting

Template plastic

*If your check isn't printed on the diagonal and you want the same look, cut squares on the bias. Be very careful not to stretch the squares when handling and sewing.

Cutting

All measurements include ¼" seam allowances. Trace triangle patterns A and B on page 20 onto template plastic and cut out on the drawn lines. Trace the templates onto the wrong side of the 3½"-wide strips as specified below, rotating the templates 180° after each cut to make the best use of your fabric. Keep like prints together as you cut.

From *each* white-with-green print fat quarter, cut:
1 strip, 5" × 21"; crosscut into 4 rectangles, 4" × 5"
    (72 total; 12 are extra)
2 strips, 3½" × 21"; crosscut into 8 A and 8 A reversed
    triangles (144 total of each)
1 strip, 2" × 21"; crosscut into 8 squares, 2" × 2"
    (144 total)

From the scraps of white-with-green prints, cut a *total* of:
4 squares, 2¼" × 2¼"

From *each* green print fat quarter, cut:
2 strips, 3½" × 21"; crosscut into:
    2 squares, 3½" × 3½" (36 total)
    8 B triangles (144 total)
1 strip, 2¼" × 21"; crosscut into 8 squares, 2¼" × 2¼"
    (144 total; 24 are extra)
1 strip, 2" × 21"; crosscut into 2 strips, 2" × 9½"
    (36 total; 12 are extra)

Continued on page 17

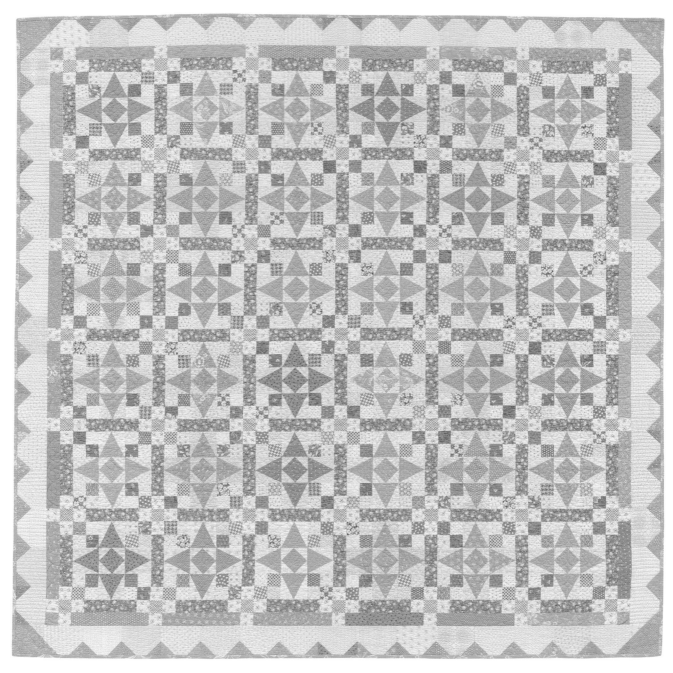

By Susan Ache; machine quilted by Susan Rogers

Quilt Size: 75" × 75" ❧ **Block Size:** 9" × 9"

Continued from page 15

From the scraps of green prints, cut a *total* of:
4 squares, 4" × 4"
4 squares, 2" × 2"

From the white floral, cut:
12 strips, 2" × 42"; crosscut 2 of the strips into
    28 squares, 2" × 2"

From the red floral, cut:
5 strips, 6½" × 42"

From the red diagonal check, cut:
3 strips, 2" × 42"; crosscut into 49 squares, 2" × 2"

From the green floral, cut:
8 strips, 2½" × 42"

Making the Blocks

Press all seam allowances as indicated by the arrows.

1. Aligning the long edges, sew a red 2" × 21" strip to a white-with-red 2" × 21" strip to make a strip set. Make 29 strip sets. Cut the strip sets into 288 segments, 2" wide.

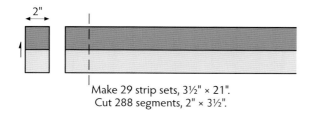

Make 29 strip sets, 3½" × 21".
Cut 288 segments, 2" × 3½".

2. Sew together two assorted segments to make a four-patch unit for the block corners. Make 144 units, each 3½" square, including seam allowances.

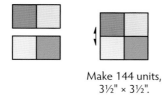

Make 144 units,
3½" × 3½".

3. Draw a diagonal line from corner to corner on the wrong side of four matching white-with-green 2" squares.

4. Place two marked white-with-green 2" squares, right sides together, on opposite corners of a green 3½" square. Sew on the drawn lines. Trim the seam allowances to ¼" and press. In the same manner, add marked squares to the remaining corners to make a block center that measures 3½" square, including seam allowances.

Make 1 unit,
3½" × 3½".

5. Using the same prints as in the unit from step 4, sew a white-with-green A triangle to one edge of a green B triangle; be sure the blunt tip of the B triangle is pointing upward. Press. Add a matching A reversed triangle to the adjacent edge of the green triangle. Make four side units that measure 3½" square, including seam allowances.

Make 4 units,
3½" × 3½".

6. Arrange and sew the block center, four side units, and four four-patch units in three rows. Join the rows to make a block that measures 9½" square, including seam allowances. Repeat to make 36 blocks.

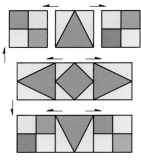

Make 36 blocks, 9½" × 9½".

Assembling the Quilt Center

1. Aligning the long edges, sew a white floral 2" × 42" strip to each side of a red floral 6½" × 42" strip to make a strip set. Make five strip sets. Cut the strip sets into 84 segments, 2" wide, for the sashing.

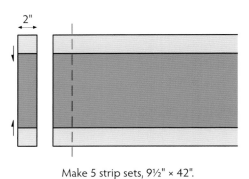

Make 5 strip sets, 9½" × 42".
Cut 84 segments, 2" × 9½".

2. Referring to the quilt assembly diagram below, lay out the blocks in six rows of six blocks each. Add the sashing pieces between the blocks and add the red check 2" squares as shown. Sew the blocks and sashing pieces into rows, and then join the rows. The quilt center should be 65" square, including seam allowances.

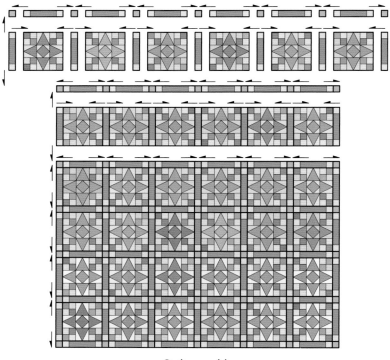

Quilt assembly

Adding the Borders

1. Sew together seven white floral 2" squares and six assorted green 2" × 9½" strips to make an inner-border strip. Make four borders that measure 2" × 65".

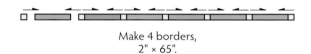

Make 4 borders,
2" × 65".

2. Add a green 2" square to each end of two of the border strips for the top and bottom inner borders. The borders should measure 2" × 68".

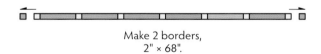

Make 2 borders,
2" × 68".

3. Draw a diagonal line from corner to corner on the wrong side of 120 green 2¼" squares and the four white-with-green 2¼" squares.

4. Place two marked green 2¼" squares, right sides together, on adjacent corners of a white-with-green 4" × 5" rectangle as shown. Sew on the drawn lines. Trim the seam allowances to ¼" and press. Make 60 border units that measure 4" × 5", including seam allowances.

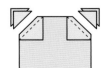

Make 60 units,
4" × 5".

5. Place a marked white-with-green 2¼" square, right sides together, on one corner of a green 4" square as shown. Sew on the drawn line. Trim the seam allowances to ¼" and press. Make four corner units that measure 4" square, including seam allowances.

Make 4 units,
4" × 4".

6. Sew together 15 border units to make an outer-border strip. Make four borders that measure 4" × 68", including seam allowances.

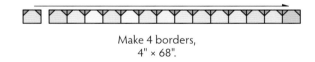

Make 4 borders,
4" × 68".

7. Add a corner unit to each end of two of the outer-border strips to make the top and bottom borders. They should measure 4" × 75", including seam allowances.

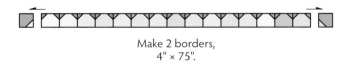

Make 2 borders,
4" × 75".

8. Sew the shorter inner-border strips to the sides of the quilt center. Sew the longer strips to the top and bottom. The quilt top should now be 68" square, including seam allowances.

9. Sew the shorter outer-border strips to the sides of the quilt center. Sew the longer strips to the top and bottom to complete the quilt top. It should measure 75" square.

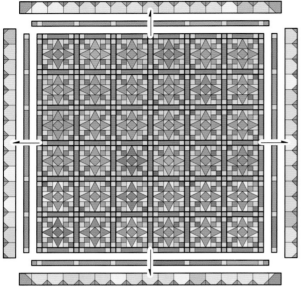

Adding the borders

Finishing the Quilt

For more details on any finishing steps, visit ShopMartingale.com/HowtoQuilt for free downloadable information.

1. Layer the backing, batting, and quilt top; baste the layers together.

2. Quilt by hand or machine. The quilt shown is machine quilted with an allover circle-and-flower design in the quilt center and inner border. The outer border is stitched with parallel straight lines in the white-with-green areas and with a pebble design in the green print.

3. Use the green floral 2½"-wide strips to make binding, and then attach the binding to the quilt.

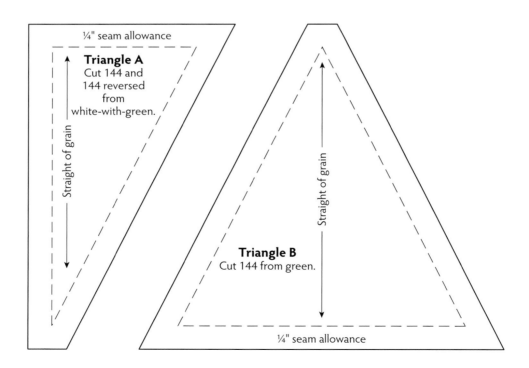

¼" seam allowance

Triangle A
Cut 144 and 144 reversed from white-with-green.

Straight of grain

Triangle B
Cut 144 from green.

Straight of grain

¼" seam allowance

SCRAPPY SISTERS

BY LISSA ALEXANDER

Here's your chance to stitch up a fabulous Lone Star-esque quilt in red and green—with added gold sparkle! The scrappy stars are easier to piece than they look, with no set-in seams. This quilt is guaranteed to help you pare down your stash. ~Lissa

Materials

Yardage is based on 42"-wide fabric.

2½ yards *total* of assorted gold prints for stars

2 yards *total* of assorted green prints for stars

2½ yards *total* of assorted white prints for stars

3 yards *total* of assorted red prints for stars

3¼ yards of white solid for setting triangles

⅞ yard of red stripe for bias binding

7¾ yards of fabric for backing

92" × 99" piece of batting

Acrylic ruler with 60° angle marking

Template plastic

Cutting

All measurements include ¼" seam allowances. Trace the triangle pattern on page 27 onto template plastic and cut out on the drawn lines. Trace the template onto the wrong side of the white solid 6½"-wide strips as specified below, rotating the template 180° after each cut to make the best use of your fabric.

From the assorted gold prints, cut a *total* of:
36 strips, 2" × 42"

From the assorted green prints, cut a *total* of:
27 strips, 2" × 42"

From the assorted white prints, cut a *total* of:
36 strips, 2" × 42"

From the assorted red prints, cut a *total* of:
45 strips, 2" × 42"

From the white solid, cut:
16 strips, 6½" × 42"; crosscut into 125 triangles

From the red stripe, cut:
360" *total* of 2½"-wide bias strips

Making the Diamond Units

Press all seam allowances as indicated by the arrows.

1. Offsetting the ends of the strips by 1" as shown, lay out and sew together one each of the gold, green, white, and red 2" × 42" strips to make strip set A. Make nine of strip set A. In the same manner, make nine each of strip sets B, C, and D.

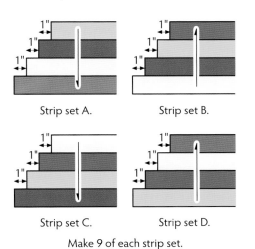

Strip set A. Strip set B.

Strip set C. Strip set D.

Make 9 of each strip set.

2. Align the 60° angle line of the ruler with the bottom of a strip set A and trim. Rotate the strip set 180° and align the 2" line of the ruler with the trimmed edge of the strip set. Cut the strip set into 15 A segments, each 2" wide. Repeat with the other A strip sets to cut a total of 125 A segments.

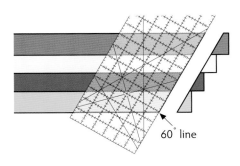

60° line

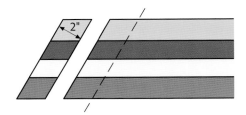

2"

Cut 125 A segments.

3. Repeat to trim each B, C, and D strip set at a 60° angle and cut 125 *each* of B, C, and D segments.

4. Aligning the seams, pin and sew together one each of segments A, B, C, and D to make a diamond unit. Press. Make 125 diamond units.

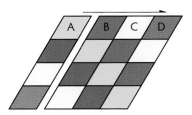

Make 125 diamond units.

Making the Blocks

1. Sew two white triangles to a diamond unit as shown to make a triangle unit. Make 45 triangle units.

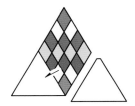 

Make 45 units.

2. Lay out one triangle unit, two diamonds units, and one white triangle in two rows as shown. Sew together the diamonds and white triangle, then sew the unit to the bottom edge of the triangle unit to make a block. Make 35 blocks.

Make 35 blocks.

By Lissa Alexander; machine quilted by Maggi Honeyman

QUILT SIZE: 83¾" × 90½"

3. Rotate a remaining triangle unit and sew a diamond unit to one white edge as shown to make a left partial block. Make five. Adding the diamond unit to the opposite corner as shown, make five right partial blocks.

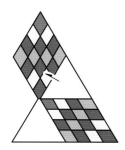

Make 5 left partial blocks.　Make 5 right partial blocks.

Assembling the Quilt Center

1. Alternating the orientation of every other block, lay out and sew together one left partial block, seven full blocks, and one right partial block to make a row. Make five rows.

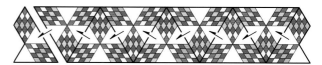

Make 5 rows.

2. Rotate every other row as shown. Matching seam intersections, sew the rows together.

Quilt assembly

3. Trim the sides of the joined rows ¼" beyond the center points of the diamond units. The trimmed quilt top should measure approximately 83¾" × 90½".

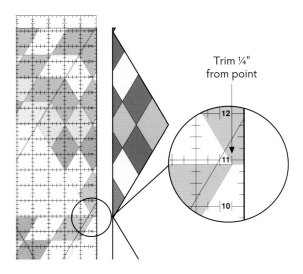

Trim ¼" from point

Finishing the Quilt

For more details on any finishing steps, visit ShopMartingale.com/HowtoQuilt for free downloadable information.

1. Layer the backing, batting, and quilt top; baste the layers together.

2. Quilt by hand or machine. The quilt shown is machine quilted with curved lines from point to point in each piece of the diamond units. A custom design of swirls and loops is quilted in the white setting triangles.

3. Use the red stripe 2½"-wide strips to make bias binding, and then attach the binding to the quilt.

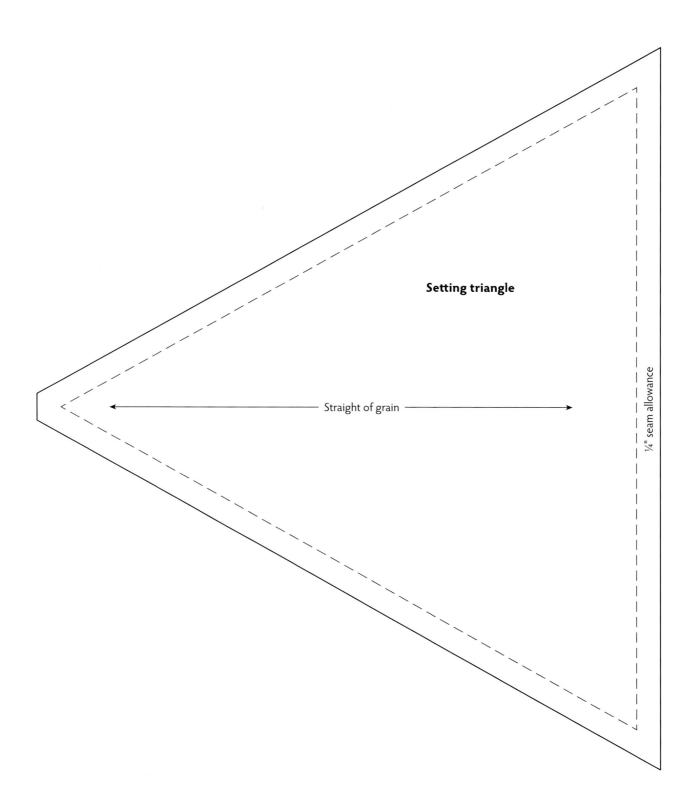

Setting triangle

Straight of grain

¼" seam allowance

HOLLY BERRY BASKETS

BY BETSY CHUTCHIAN

Basket blocks are among my favorites. Gather some red, green, and cheddar prints to stitch in varying combinations with a cream background. I've combined the baskets with classic Nine Patch blocks to create a lively quilt I'm happy to add to my collection. ~Betsy

Materials

Yardage is based on 42"-wide fabric.

2⅝ yards of cream solid for blocks, sashing, and nine-patch sashing units

¼ yard *each* of 4 green prints for blocks (label them #1–4)

⅜ yard of green print #5 for blocks

⅜ yard of red print #1 for blocks

⅛ yard *each* of 3 red prints for blocks (label them #2–4)

¼ yard of cheddar print for blocks

½ yard of green tone on tone for blocks and nine-patch sashing units

1⅞ yards of red-with-white print for blocks, sashing, setting triangles, and binding

3⅛ yards of fabric for backing

55" × 67" piece of batting

Cutting

All measurements include ¼" seam allowances.

From the cream solid, cut:

5 strips, 6¾" × 42"; crosscut into 160 strips, 1¼" × 6¾"

3 strips, 5⅞" × 42"; crosscut into 16 squares, 5⅞" × 5⅞". Cut in half diagonally to make 32 triangles.

3 strips, 4¼" × 42"; crosscut into 64 rectangles, 1¾" × 4¼"

2 strips, 3⅜" × 42"; crosscut into 16 squares, 3⅜" × 3⅜". Cut in half diagonally to make 32 triangles.

2 strips, 2¼" × 42"; crosscut into 30 squares, 2¼" × 2¼"

7 strips, 1¼" × 42"

From *each* of green prints #1–4, cut:

1 rectangle, 6" × 11"; cut diagonally into 4 bias strips, ¾" × 8" (16 total)

From the *remainder* of each green print #1–4, cut:

12 squares, 2¼" × 2¼" (48 total)

12 squares, 2⅛" × 2⅛"; cut in half diagonally to make 24 triangles (96 total)

Continued on page 31

By Betsy Chutchian; machine quilted by Maggi Honeyman

QUILT SIZE: 48½" × 60½" ❧ **BLOCK SIZE:** 6¼" × 6¼"

Continued from page 29

From green print #5, cut:
1 rectangle, 6" × 13½"; cut diagonally into 6 bias
  strips, ¾" × 8"
1 strip, 2¼" × 42"; crosscut into 18 squares, 2¼" × 2¼"
1 strip, 2⅛" × 42"; crosscut into 18 squares, 2⅛" × 2⅛".
  Cut in half diagonally to make 36 triangles.

From red print #1, cut:
1 rectangle, 6" × 13½"; cut diagonally into 6 bias
  strips, ¾" × 8"
1 strip, 2¼" × 42"; crosscut into 18 squares, 2¼" × 2¼"
1 strip, 2⅛" × 42"; crosscut into 18 squares, 2⅛" × 2⅛".
  Cut in half diagonally to make 36 triangles.

From *each* of red prints #2–4, cut:
1 strip, 2¼" × 42"; crosscut into 12 squares, 2¼" × 2¼"
  (36 total)

From the green tone on tone, cut:
7 strips, 1¼" × 42"; crosscut *1* of the strips into
  18 squares, 1¼" × 1¼"
1 rectangle, 6" × 11"; cut diagonally into 4 bias strips,
  ¾" × 8"

From the cheddar print, cut:
2 strips, 2¼" × 42"; crosscut into 18 squares, 2¼" × 2¼"

From the *remainder* of the green tone on tone, cut:
12 squares, 2¼" × 2¼"
12 squares, 2⅛" × 2⅛"; cut in half diagonally to make
  24 triangles

From the red-with-white print, cut:
2 strips, 10¼" × 42"; crosscut into:*
  4 squares, 10¼" × 10¼"; cut into quarters
    diagonally to make 16 triangles (2 are extra)
  2 squares, 5½" × 5½"; cut in half diagonally to
    make 4 triangles
3 strips, 6¾" × 42"; crosscut into 80 strips, 1¼" × 6¾"
6 strips, 2½" × 42"
1 strip, 2¼" × 42"; crosscut into 12 squares, 2¼" × 2¼"
2 strips, 1¼" × 42"

**If your fabric is wide enough, you may be able to cut
the four 10¼" squares from one 10¼" strip. If that's the
case, cut a 5½" × 42" strip for the 5½" squares, or cut
them from the remainder of the fabric after all other
strips are cut.*

Appliquéing the Handles

For more information on appliqué techniques, go to
ShopMartingale.com/HowtoQuilt.

1. Press under a scant ¼" on the long edges of each
green and red ¾"-wide bias strip to prepare 32
handles for appliqué.

2. Using a pencil, trace the handle placement on the
pattern on page 35 lightly on each cream 5⅞" triangle
with a pencil.

3. Baste and appliqué each handle to a cream
triangle to make 32 handle units. Trim any excess
length from the handle even with the edge of the
triangle.

Make 32 units.

Making Half-Square-Triangle Units

Press all seam allowances as indicated by the arrows.

1. Draw a diagonal line from corner to corner on the wrong side of 12 cream 2¼" squares.

2. Layer a marked 2¼" square on a 2¼" green #1 square, right sides together. Stitch a scant ¼" from both sides of the marked line. Cut on the line to make two half-square-triangle units. Trim the units to 1¾" square. Make 24 units.

Make 24 units.

3. Repeat steps 1 and 2 to make 168 half-square-triangle units as follows. Draw the diagonal line on the lighter fabric in each pair.

- 36 of red #1 and cream
- 36 of green #5 and cheddar
- 24 of green #2 and red #2
- 24 of green #3 and red #3
- 24 of green #4 and red #4
- 24 of green tone on tone and red-with-white print

Making the Basket Blocks

1. Lay out four 2⅛" green #1 triangles and six cream/green #1 half-square-triangle units in four rows. Sew together the pieces in each row. Join the rows to make a basket unit. Press as shown, referring to "Pressing Advice" above right to press the seam intersections open. Make four matching basket units.

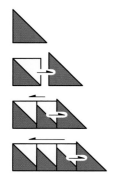

Make 4 units.

❧ Pressing Advice ❧

Where multiple seams meet, clip into the seam allowance ¼" from the intersecting seam and flip the seam allowances to create the least amount of bulk. Then press the unit.

2. Sew a green #1 handle unit to a basket unit. Make four units, each 5½" square.

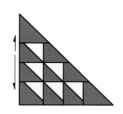

Make 4 units,
5½" × 5½".

3. Sew a 2⅛" green #1 triangle to a cream 1¾" × 4¼" rectangle as shown to make a left base unit. Repeat to make a right base unit with the triangle facing the opposite direction. Sew the base units to a basket unit. Then add a cream 3⅜" triangle to complete a Basket block that measures 6¾" square, including seam allowances. Make four green #1/cream blocks.

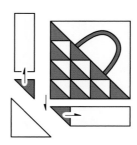 

Make 4 blocks,
6¾" × 6¾".

4. Repeat steps 1–3 to make 28 blocks with cream backgrounds as follows:

- 6 using red #1 triangles and red #1/cream half-square-triangle units
- 4 using green #2 triangles and green #2/red #2 half-square-triangle units
- 4 using green #3 triangles and green #3/red #3 half-square-triangle units
- 4 using green #4 triangles and green #4/red #4 half-square-triangle units
- 4 using green tone on tone triangles and green tone-on-tone/red-and-white print half-square-triangle units
- 6 using green #5 triangles and green #5/cheddar half-square-triangle units

Make 6 red-and-cream blocks, 6¾" × 6¾".

Make 16 green-and-red blocks, 6¾" × 6¾".

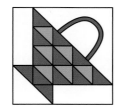

Make 6 green-and-cheddar blocks, 6¾" × 6¾".

Making the Sashing Units

1. Sew together two cream 1¼" × 6¾" strips and one red-with-white 1¼" × 6¾" strip to make a sashing rectangle that is 2¾" × 6¾", including seam allowances. Make 80 sashing rectangles.

Make 80 sashing rectangles, 2¾" × 6¾".

2. Aligning the long edges, sew together two green tone-on-tone 1¼" × 42" strips and one cream 1¼" × 42" strip to make strip set A measuring 2¾" × 42". Make three A strip sets. Cut the strip sets into 80 A segments, 1¼" wide.

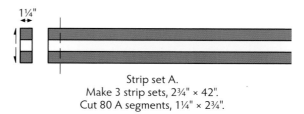

Strip set A.
Make 3 strip sets, 2¾" × 42".
Cut 80 A segments, 1¼" × 2¾".

3. Aligning the long edges, sew together two cream 1¼" × 42" strips and one red-with-white 1¼" × 42" strip to make strip set B. Make two B strip sets. Cut the strip sets into 49 B segments, 1¼" wide.

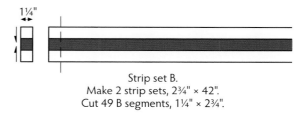

Strip set B.
Make 2 strip sets, 2¾" × 42".
Cut 49 B segments, 1¼" × 2¾".

4. Sew together two A segments and one B segment to make a nine-patch unit that measures 2¾" square, including seam allowances. Make 31.

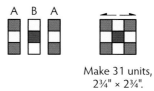

Make 31 units, 2¾" × 2¾".

5. Sew together one A segment, one B segment, and one green tone-on-tone 1¼" square to make a partial nine-patch unit. Make 18.

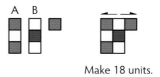

Make 18 units.

Assembling the Quilt Top

1. Lay out the blocks, nine-patch units, partial nine-patch units, sashing rectangles, and side setting triangles in diagonal rows as shown in the quilt assembly diagram below.

2. Sew the pieces into rows, then join the rows. Add the corner triangles to each corner of the quilt top. Trim the setting triangles and the partial nine-patch units ¼" beyond the center of the partial

nine-patch units as shown below to complete the quilt top, which should measure 48½" × 60½".

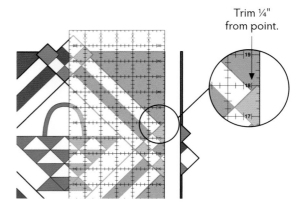

Trim ¼" from point.

Quilt assembly

Finishing the Quilt

For more details on any finishing steps, visit ShopMartingale.com/HowtoQuilt for free downloadable information.

1. Layer the backing, batting, and quilt top; baste the layers together.

2. Quilt by hand or machine. The quilt shown is machine quilted with assorted swirls and shells in the blocks and quilted in the ditch in the nine-patch units.

3. Use the red-with-white print 2½"-wide strips to make binding, and then attach the binding to the quilt.

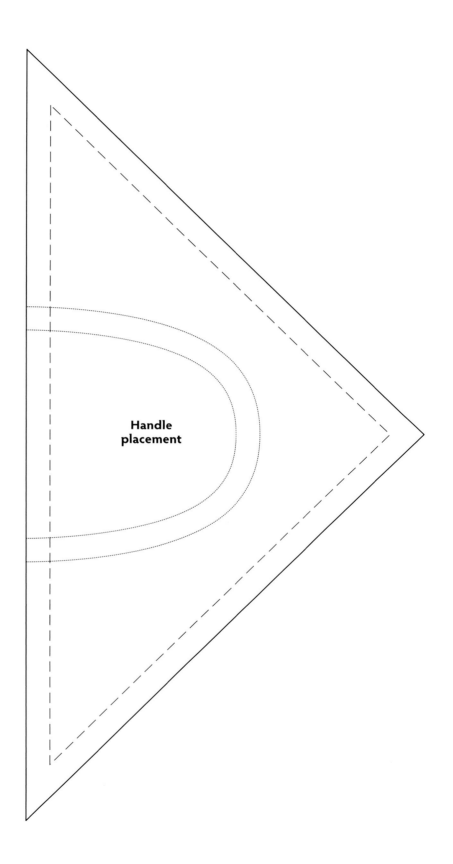

Handle placement

WINTERBERRIES

BY JO MORTON

I've always loved the combination of piecing and appliqué. As is often the case, this quilt was inspired by an antique bed quilt. The appliqué design really caught my eye and seemed perfect for a red-and-green interpretation. The cheddar sashing squares add a touch of old-time charm. ~Jo

Materials

Yardage is based on 42"-wide fabric.

2⅞ yards of cream print for blocks and setting triangles

1½ yards *total* of assorted red prints for pieced blocks and appliqués

1 yard *total* of assorted green prints for appliqués

¼ yard of cheddar print for sashing squares

1 yard of green stripe for sashing and single-fold binding (You'll need 1¼ yards if you prefer double-fold binding.)

3⅛ yards of fabric for backing

56" × 56" piece of batting

Template plastic

Cutting

All measurements include ¼" seam allowances.

From the cream print, cut:

2 strips, 12" × 42"; crosscut into 4 squares, 12" × 12"

4 strips, 7" × 42"; crosscut into 18 squares, 7" × 7"

5 strips, 3¼" × 42"; crosscut into 50 squares, 3¼" × 3¼". Cut squares into quarters diagonally to make 200 triangles.

4 strips, 2⅜" × 42"; crosscut into 50 squares, 2⅜" × 2⅜"

3 strips, 2⅛" × 42"; crosscut into 50 squares, 2⅛" × 2⅛". Cut squares in half diagonally to make 100 triangles.

2 strips, 2" × 42"; crosscut into 25 squares, 2" × 2"

From the assorted red prints, cut:

25 *matching sets* of:
    4 rectangles, 2" × 3¼" (100 total)
    2 squares, 2⅜" × 2⅜" (50 total)

16 squares, 4" × 4"

20 rectangles, 2" × 5"

Continued on page 39

By Jo Morton; appliquéd by Kathy Hall; machine quilted by Lori Kukuk

Quilt Size: 50" × 50" ❧ **Block Size:** 6" × 6"

Continued from page 37

From the assorted green prints, cut:
16 squares, 6½" × 6½"
16 rectangles, 3" × 4½"

From the cheddar print, cut:
3 strips, 1½" × 42"; crosscut into 60 squares, 1½" × 1½"

From the green stripe, cut:
17 strips, 1½" × 42"; crosscut into 100 rectangles,
    1½" × 6½"
6 strips, 1⅛" × 42"

Making the Pieced Blocks

Press all seam allowances as indicated by the arrows.

1. Draw a diagonal line from corner to corner on the wrong side of each cream 2⅜" square.

2. Layer a marked square on a red 2⅜" square, right sides together. Stitch a scant ¼" from both sides of the marked line. Cut on the line to make two half-square-triangle units. Trim the units to 1⅞" square. Make four matching units.

Make 4 units.

3. Sew a cream 3¼" triangle to each red edge of a half-square-triangle unit to make a side triangle unit. Make four units.

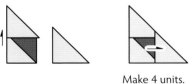

Make 4 units.

4. Lay out four matching red 2" × 3¼" rectangles, four side triangle units, one cream 2" square, and four cream 2⅛" triangles in diagonal rows as shown above right. Sew together the pieces in each row; join the rows. Add the cream triangles to the corners. Press as

shown, referring to "Pressing Advice" on page 32 to press the center seam intersections open. Centering the block, trim to 6½" square. Make 25 blocks.

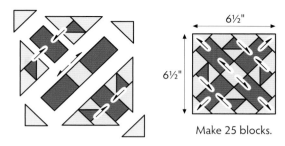

Make 25 blocks.

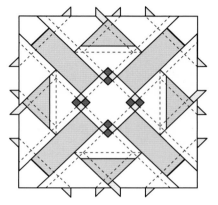

Appliquéing the Blocks and Triangles

Jo used the back-basting appliqué method for her quilt. This method is reflected in the following steps. Feel free to use your own favorite appliqué technique. For more information on appliqué techniques, go to ShopMartingale.com/HowtoQuilt.

1. Trace the block design on page 42 onto the wrong side of 16 cream 7" squares. (Set aside the remaining two squares for the corner setting triangles.)

2. Center a green 6½" square right side up on the right side of a marked background square. Pin in place. Follow the traced lines on the wrong side to baste the green fabric in place around the A leaves and the inner openings. Trim the green fabric ⅛" away from the basting around the outer edges of the leaves and carefully cut a slit in the center of the leaf openings. Working an inch or so at a time, remove the basting and use the holes left behind as a guide to turn under the seam allowances and appliqué in place, clipping into the seam allowances as necessary.

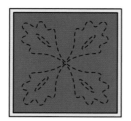

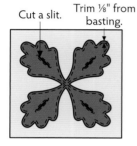

3. Using a red 4" square, repeat step 2 to baste and appliqué each set of four B leaves. Centering the design, trim the block to 6½" square, including seam allowances. Make 16 appliquéd blocks.

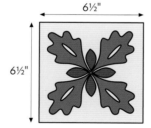

Make 16 blocks.

4. In the same manner as step 3, make a template for the side triangle appliqué using the pattern on page 43 and trace it four times onto the wrong side of each cream 12" square. Then use a ruler to draw a ¼" seam allowance around each traced triangle. Using the green 3" × 4½" rectangles and the remaining red 2" × 5" rectangles, appliqué the C and D shapes in place on each triangle in the same

manner as for the blocks. Cut the triangles along the outer lines to make 16 side setting triangles.

Make 16 side setting triangles.

5. Trace the entire corner triangle pattern on page 43 (the triangle shape and the D leaves) onto template plastic and cut it out. Using the template, trace two triangle shapes and the D shapes for each onto the wrong side of each remaining cream 7" square, leaving space around each edge for a seam allowance. Using a ruler, draw a ¼" seam allowance around each traced triangle. Using the red 2" × 5" rectangles, appliqué the leaves in place on each triangle in the same manner as the blocks. Cut the triangles on the outer lines to make the four corner setting triangles.

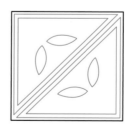
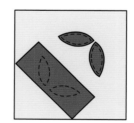

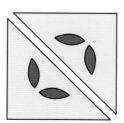

Make 4 corner triangles.

Assembling the Quilt Top

1. Lay out the blocks, cheddar 1½" squares, green stripe 1½" × 6½" rectangles, and side setting triangles in diagonal rows as shown in the quilt assembly diagram below.

2. Sew together the pieces in each sashing row. Then join the pieces in each block row. Sew the adjacent sashing rows to each block row before adding the side setting triangles. Join all of the rows. Add the corner triangles to each corner. Trim the setting triangles and cheddar squares ¼" beyond the center of the cheddar squares. The quilt top should measure 50" square.

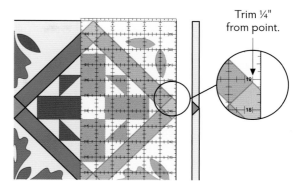

Trim ¼" from point.

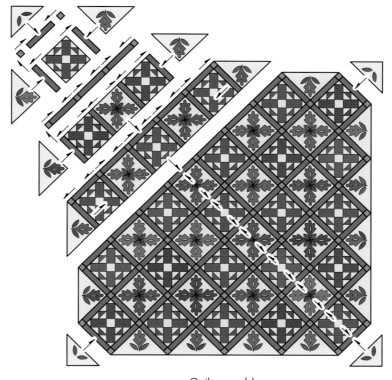

Quilt assembly

Finishing the Quilt

For more details on any finishing steps, visit ShopMartingale.com/HowtoQuilt for free downloadable information.

1. Layer the backing, batting, and quilt top; baste the layers together.

2. Quilt by hand or machine. The quilt shown is machine quilted in the ditch of each block edge and through the center of each sashing row. The pieced blocks are quilted in the ditch and with a loopy continuous line in the rectangles. For the appliquéd blocks, echo quilting about ¼" apart surrounds the green leaves. Green quilting about ¼" inside each green leaf and a line of red quilting in each red leaf gives the leaves definition and keeps them from puffing up.

3. Use the green stripe 1⅛"-wide strips to make single-fold binding, and then attach the binding to the quilt.

Block appliqué pattern

Corner triangle appliqué pattern

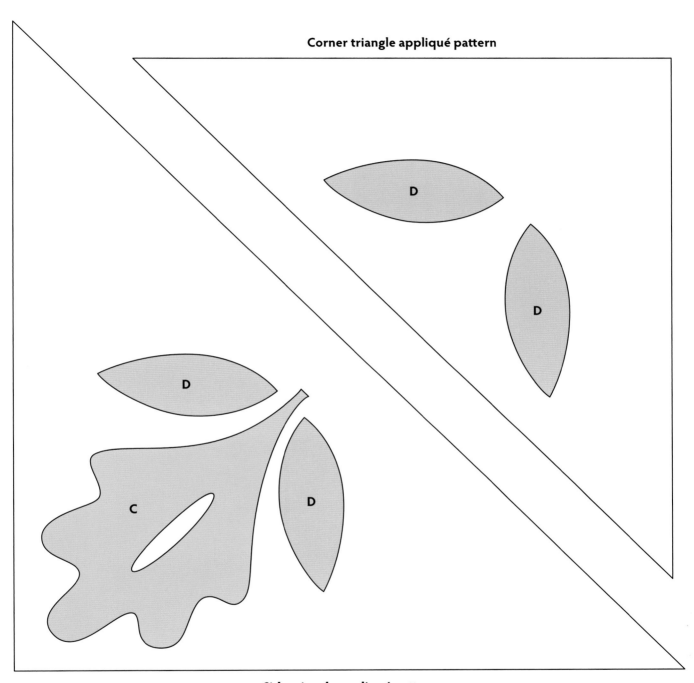

Side triangle appliqué pattern

Appliqué patterns do not
include seam allowances.

HOLLY BEARS THE CROWN

BY SANDY KLOP

I pulled out all the stops and enjoyed creating this red-and-green quilt. I included many of my favorite holiday images—twinkling stars, holly leaves and berries, and a peppermint twist border. It doesn't get any better than that! ~Sandy

Materials

Yardage is based on 42"-wide fabric.

⅓ yard of green paisley for stars

7 yards of cream tone on tone for stars, background, and borders

2⅛ yards of red floral for stars, pieced border, and binding

¼ yard of gold print for stars

½ yard *total* of assorted green prints for appliqués

⅛ yard *total* of assorted red prints for appliqués

⅜ yard of green dot for inner border

7⅝ yards of fabric for backing

91" × 91" piece of batting

Acrylic ruler with 45° angle

Template plastic

Cutting

All measurements include ¼" seam allowances. Trace the A and B diamond patterns on page 54 onto template plastic and cut out on the drawn lines. Trace the templates onto the wrong side of the strips as specified below.

From the green paisley, cut:
4 strips, 2" × 42"

From the red floral, cut:
9 strips, 2½" × 42"
7 strips, 2⅛" × 42"; crosscut *1* of the strips into 4 B diamonds
15 strips, 2" × 42"; crosscut *2* of the strips into 16 A diamonds
1 square, 3⅛" × 3⅛"; cut in half diagonally to make 2 triangles

From the gold print, cut:
3 strips, 2" × 42"

From the green dot, cut:
6 strips, 1½" × 42"

Continued on page 47

By Sandy Klop; machine quilted by Nancy Connolly

QUILT SIZE: 82½" × 82½"

Continued from page 45

From the *lengthwise* grain of the cream tone on tone, cut:

2 strips, 9⅝" × 78¾"

2 strips, 9⅝" × 60½"

From the remaining cream tone on tone, cut:

2 strips, 17½" × 42"; crosscut into:
    1 square, 17½" × 17½"
    4 rectangles, 9" × 17½"

2 strips, 9" × 42"; crosscut into 8 squares, 9" × 9"

1 strip, 13¼" × 42"; crosscut into 2 squares,
    13¼" × 13¼". Cut into quarters diagonally to
    make 8 triangles.

3 strips, 5" × 42"

3 strips, 3½" × 42"

7 strips, 2⅛" × 42"; crosscut *1* of the strips into
    4 B diamonds

20 strips, 2" × 42"; crosscut *3* of the strips into
    32 A diamonds

1 square, 3⅛" × 3⅛"; cut in half diagonally to
    make 2 triangles

Making the Stars

Press all seam allowances as indicated by the arrows.

1. Aligning the long edges, lay out and sew together one green paisley, one red floral, and two cream 2" × 42" strips to make strip set A. Make four strip sets.

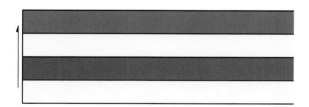

Strip set A.
Make 4 strip sets,
6½" × 42".

2. Align the 45° angle line of the ruler with the bottom of a strip set and trim. Rotate the strip set 180° and align the 2" line of the ruler with the trimmed edge of the strip set. Cut the strip set into 11 segments, each 2" wide. Repeat to cut a total of 40 A segments.

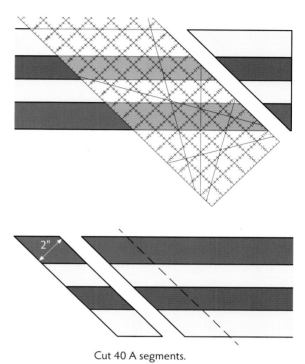

Cut 40 A segments.

3. In the same manner as for strip set A, make three each of strip sets B, C, and D as follows.

- Strip set B: one cream 2" × 42" strip, one red 2" × 42" strip, and one cream 3½" × 42" strip
- Strip set C: two red and two cream 2" × 42" strips
- Strip set D: one cream 5" × 42" strip and one gold 2" × 42" strip

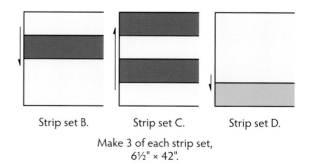

Strip set B.   Strip set C.   Strip set D.

Make 3 of each strip set,
6½" × 42".

4. Repeat step 2 to trim each strip set at a 45° angle. Cut 32 segments, 2" wide, from each of the B, C, and D strip sets.

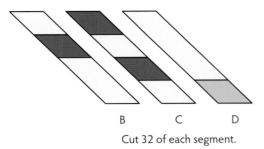

Cut 32 of each segment.

5. Aligning the seams, pin and sew together one each of segments A, B, C, and D to make a diamond unit. Press. Make 32 diamond units. (You'll have eight additional A segments to be used in the center block.)

Make 32 diamond units.

6. Starting and stopping ¼" from the beginning and end of the seams as shown by the dots, sew together two diamond units to make a quarter star. Make 16 quarter stars.

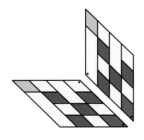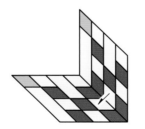

Make 16 quarter stars.

7. In the same manner, sew together two quarter stars to make a half star. Make eight half stars. Join the half stars to make four stars.

Make 4 stars.

Making the Center Block

1. Lay out one A segment, four cream A diamonds, and two red A diamonds in four rows as shown. Sew together the diamonds in each row and join the rows to make a half diamond. Make eight half diamonds.

Make 8 half-diamond units.

2. Starting and stopping ¼" from the beginning and end of each seam, sew together the half diamonds into quarters and then halves. Join the halves to complete the star.

Make 1 center star unit.

3. Mark a 16¾"-diameter circle on the center star unit by measuring 8⅜" from the center and making a pencil mark. Repeat this around the star and then draw a circle to connect the marks.

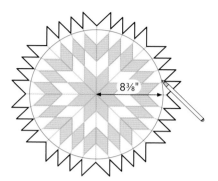

Draw a circle 16¾" in diameter.

4. Stay stitch around the star just inside the drawn line and then trim on the drawn lines to create a circle.

5. Fold the cream 17½" square in half in both directions and finger-press lightly to mark the center. Repeat, folding in half diagonally in both directions. Position and pin the star on the background square, centering it on the pressed lines.

6. Carefully turning under the edges ¼", appliqué the star to the background to complete the center block. (For more information on appliqué techniques, go to ShopMartingale.com/HowtoQuilt.)

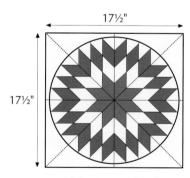

Make 1 center block.

Appliquéing the Setting Pieces and Borders

1. Using the patterns on page 54 and adding ¼" seam allowances, cut out 20 large leaves, 12 reversed large leaves, and eight small leaves from the assorted green prints; cut out 28 small berries, four medium berries, and four large berries from the assorted red prints.

2. Referring to the appliqué placement diagram below and the photo on page 46, appliqué one large leaf, one reversed large leaf, one small leaf, and three small berries on a cream 9" setting square. Appliqué eight setting squares.

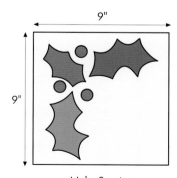

Make 8 units.

3. Appliqué a large leaf on a cream 13¼" setting triangle. Make eight setting triangles.

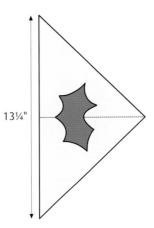

13¼"

Make 8 units.

4. Fold the 9⅝"-wide cream border strips (either length) in half to mark their centers. Appliqué one large leaf, one reversed large leaf, one small berry, one medium berry, and one large berry to each border strip as shown (referring to the photo on page 46 as needed for placement guidance).

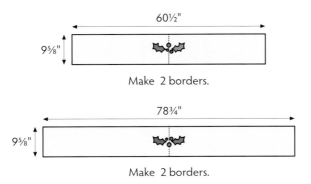

60½"

9⅝"

Make 2 borders.

78¾"

9⅝"

Make 2 borders.

Assembling the Quilt Center

Use set-in seams (see page 51) to assemble the quilt center. Press the seam allowances open or in the directions that will allow them to lie the flattest.

1. Lay out the stars, center block, setting squares and triangles, and cream 9" × 17½" rectangles as shown in the quilt assembly diagram on page 51.

2. Sew a cream setting triangle to a star by aligning one short edge of the triangle with the pieced diamond. Begin sewing at the outer edge and stitch to the inner point, stopping ¼" from the end. With the needle down, raise the presser foot and pivot the fabrics to align the next edge of the cream triangle with the adjacent diamond. Stitch from the center to the outside edge.

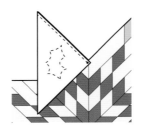
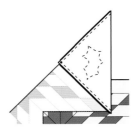

3. Set in a second triangle and the corner square. Repeat with the remaining large stars.

❧ Set-In Seams ❧

Set-in seams enable you to insert pieces such as squares and triangles into an angled opening. When setting in seams, do not stitch into the seam allowances of the angled opening. Start and stop exactly at the point where the ¼" seam allowances intersect.

---

4. Join the stars in pairs horizontally, setting in the cream square between them. Take care that the appliquéd holly leaves are in the correct position when insetting the squares.

5. Set in a cream rectangle between each pair of stars.

6. Join the two pairs of stars, setting in the remaining squares and cream rectangles between them.

7. Set in the center block. The quilt top should measure 58½" square, including seam allowances.

Adding the Borders

1. Aligning the long edges, sew together one red 2⅛" × 42" strip and one cream 2⅛" × 42" strip to make a strip set. Make six strip sets.

Make 6 strip sets,
3¾" × 42".

2. In the same manner as for the diamond units, trim one end of three strip sets at a 45° angle and cut into 32 segments, each 2⅛" wide.

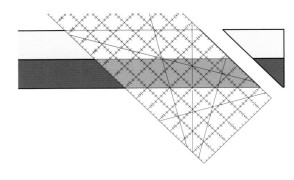

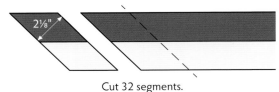

Cut 32 segments.

3. Angling the ruler in the opposite direction, trim one end of three strip sets at a 45° angle and cut into 32 reversed segments, each 2⅛" wide.

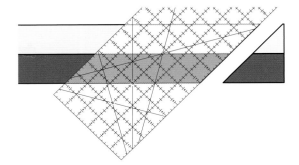

Cut 32 reversed segments.

4. Lay out and sew together eight reversed segments, two cream B diamonds, one red 3⅛" triangle, and eight segments in a row. Make two top/bottom borders.

Make 2 top/bottom borders.

5. Rotating the segments as shown, lay out and sew together eight segments, two red B diamonds, one cream 3⅛" triangle, and eight reversed segments in a row. Make two side borders.

Make 2 side borders.

6. Join the green dot 1½" × 42" strips end to end and press the seam allowances open. Trim the pieced length into two 60½"-long inner-border strips and two 58½"-long inner-border strips. Sew the shorter strips to opposite edges of the quilt center. Sew the longer strips to the remaining edges. The quilt top should now be 60½" square, including seam allowances.

7. Sew the short appliquéd middle border strips to opposite edges of the quilt center. Add the long appliquéd middle border strips to the remaining edges. The quilt top should now be 78¾" square, including seam allowances.

8. Starting and stopping the seams ¼" from the ends, sew the top/bottom outer-border strips to opposite edges of the quilt top; pay attention to the direction of the diamonds and center triangle. Sew the side outer-border strips to the remaining edges of the quilt, setting in the corners, to complete the quilt top, which should measure 82½" square.

Finishing the Quilt

For more details on any finishing steps, visit ShopMartingale.com/HowtoQuilt for free downloadable information.

1. Layer the backing, batting, and quilt top; baste the layers together.

2. Quilt by hand or machine. The quilt shown is machine quilted with an allover spiral, holly leaf, and berry design in the quilt center and with a spiral and feather design in the middle border.

3. Use the red floral 2½"-wide strips to make binding, and then attach the binding to the quilt.

Adding the borders

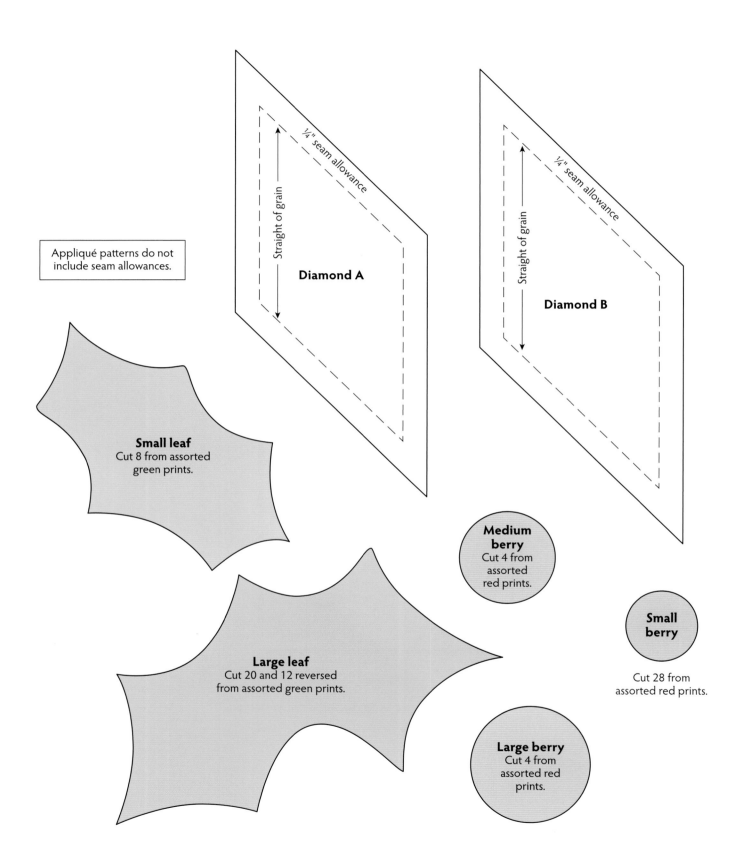

Appliqué patterns do not include seam allowances.

Diamond A

Diamond B

¼" seam allowance

Straight of grain

Small leaf
Cut 8 from assorted green prints.

Medium berry
Cut 4 from assorted red prints.

Small berry
Cut 28 from assorted red prints.

Large leaf
Cut 20 and 12 reversed from assorted green prints.

Large berry
Cut 4 from assorted red prints.

Snow Lilies

BY CAROL HOPKINS

Scraps of red and green fabrics, augmented with bits of cheddar, may be a humble beginning, but the result is anything but ordinary. The floral bouquets set against a snowy background will impart a sense of calm beauty in any room at any time of year. ~Carol

Materials

Yardage is based on 42"-wide fabric.

8 assorted cheddar print scraps, at least 4" × 16" each, for blocks

16 assorted red print scraps, at least 6" × 16" each, for blocks and pieced border

16 assorted green print scraps, at least 6" × 13" each, for blocks

5¼ yards of cream solid for blocks and borders

½ yard of red print for binding

3⅝ yards of fabric for backing

66" × 76" piece of batting

Cutting

All measurements include ¼" seam allowances. Keep like pieces together as you cut.

From *each* of the cheddar print scraps, cut:
12 squares, 1½" × 1½" (96 total)

From *each* of the red print scraps, cut:
11 squares, 2½" × 2½"; cut 5 of the squares in half diagonally to make 10 triangles (96 squares total and 160 triangles total; 18 triangles are extra)

From *each* of the green print scraps, cut:
12 squares, 2" × 2"; cut the squares in half diagonally to make 24 triangles (384 total)
8 squares, 1½" × 1½" (128 total)

From the *lengthwise* grain of the cream solid, cut:
4 strips, 4½" × 66"
11 strips, 1½" × 66"; crosscut into:
    1 strip, 1½" × 65½"
    2 strips, 1½" × 57½"
    2 strips, 1½" × 41½"
    2 strips, 1½" × 25½"
    2 strips, 1½" × 9½"
    40 strips, 1½" × 7½"

Continued on page 57

Continued from page 55

From the remaining cream solid, cut:

2 strips, 14" × 42"; crosscut into:
  4 squares, 14" × 14"; cut into quarters diagonally
    to make 16 triangles (2 are extra)
  2 squares, 9" × 9"; cut in half diagonally to make
    4 triangles
5 strips, 2½" × 42"; crosscut into 71 squares,
  2½" × 2½". Cut in half diagonally to make
  142 triangles.
10 strips, 2" × 42"; crosscut into 196 squares, 2" × 2".
  Cut *192* of the squares in half diagonally to make
  384 triangles.
23 strips, 1½" × 42"; crosscut into:
  128 rectangles, 1½" × 3½"
  64 rectangles, 1½" × 2½"
  160 squares, 1½" × 1½"

From the red print for binding, cut:

7 strips, 2" × 42"

Making the Blocks

Press all seam allowances as indicated by the arrows. Each block contains one red, one green, and one cheddar print; select pieces from matching prints for all of the units in one block.

1. Draw a diagonal line from corner to corner on the wrong side of three cheddar 1½" squares.

2. Place a marked cheddar 1½" square on one corner of a red 2½" square, right sides together. Sew on the marked line. Fold the resulting triangle along the sewing line toward the corner and press. If desired, trim the excess corner fabric ¼" from the stitched line. Make three units measuring 2½" square, including seam allowances.

Make 3 units,
2½" × 2½".

3. Sew 12 green and 12 cream 2" triangles together in pairs to make 12 half-square-triangle units. Trim each unit to 1½" square.

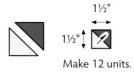

Make 12 units.

4. Join two half-square-triangle units to make a unit measuring 1½" × 2½", including seam allowances. Make three units.

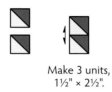

Make 3 units,
1½" × 2½".

5. Join two half-square-triangle units and a cream 1½" square to make a unit measuring 1½" × 3½", including seam allowances. Make three units.

Make 3 units,
1½" × 3½".

6. Sew a step 4 unit to the left edge of a step 2 unit as shown. Then add a step 5 unit to the top edge to make a flower unit, making sure the units are oriented in the correct direction. The unit should be 3½" square, including seam allowances. Make three flower units.

Make 3 units,
3½" × 3½".

By Carol Hopkins; machine quilted by Ruth Wasmuth

QUILT SIZE: 59½" × 70" ❧ **BLOCK SIZE:** 7" × 7"

7. Arrange and sew two cream and two green 1½" squares in two rows. Join the rows to make a four-patch unit measuring 2½" square, including seam allowances.

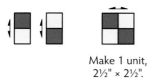

Make 1 unit,
2½" × 2½".

8. Arrange and sew one green 1½" square, two cream 1½" × 2½" rectangles, and the four-patch unit in two rows. Join the rows to make a stem unit measuring 3½" square, including seam allowances.

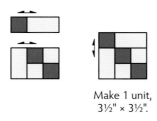

Make 1 unit,
3½" × 3½".

9. Lay out and sew three flower units, four cream 1½" × 3½" rectangles, the stem unit, and one green 1½" square in three rows as shown. Join the rows to make a block measuring 7½" square, including seam allowances. Make 32 blocks.

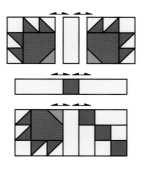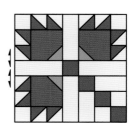

Make 32 blocks,
7½" × 7½".

Assembling the Quilt Center

1. Lay out the blocks, cream 1½"-wide strips, and cream side setting triangles in diagonal rows as shown. The setting triangles are cut oversized to allow for trimming before adding the pieced borders.

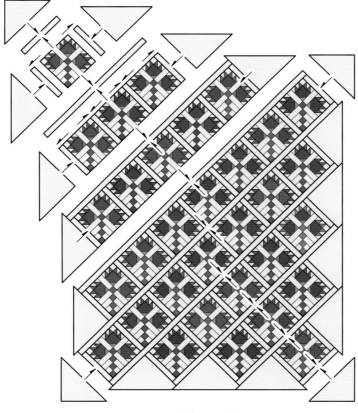

Quilt assembly

2. Sew the pieces into rows, then join the rows. Add the corner triangles to each corner. You will need to trim and square up the quilt top, but you may want to wait until you've pieced the inner borders to make sure they will both be the same length. The quilt top should measure 48½" x 59", including seam allowances, to accommodate an accurately pieced inner border.

Trimming diagram

Adding the Borders

1. Sew cream and assorted red 2½" triangles together in pairs to make 142 half-square-triangle units. Trim each unit to 2" square.

Make 142 units.

2. Sew together 39 half-square-triangle units to make a side border that measures 2" × 59", including seam allowances. Make two.

Make 2 borders,
2" × 59".

3. Join two cream 2" squares and 32 half-square triangle units to make the top border, which should be 2" × 51½", including seam allowances. Repeat to make the bottom border.

Make 2 borders,
2" × 51½".

4. Sew the side pieced borders to the quilt top and then add the top and bottom pieced borders.

5. Measure the length of the quilt top through the center and trim two of the cream 4½"-wide strips to this measurement. Sew the strips to the sides of the quilt and press.

❧ Putting It All Together ❧

For pieced borders to mathematically fit the quilt center, you may need to adjust the length of the border strips. The easiest and least noticeable way to match the border lengths to the quilt top is by making some of the seam allowances a tiny bit smaller. Or, you may need to ease the quilt top to fit the borders.

---

6. Measure the width of the quilt top through the center, including the borders just added, and trim the two remaining cream 4½"-wide strips to this measurement. Sew the strips to the top and bottom of the quilt and press to complete the quilt top, which should measure 59½" × 70".

Adding the borders

Finishing the Quilt

For more details on any finishing steps, visit ShopMartingale.com/HowtoQuilt for free downloadable information.

1. Layer the backing, batting, and quilt top; baste the layers together.

2. Quilt by hand or machine. The quilt shown is machine quilted with stippling around the lilies and feathers in the borders and setting triangles.

3. Use the red print 2"-wide strips to make binding, and then attach the binding to the quilt.

STAR FROND

BY COREY YODER

My vision for a red–and–green quilt was simple but elegant. Both the piecing and appliqué are easy, leaving ample space for beautiful quilting. Hang this stunner on the wall, or make it larger with additional blocks for a beautiful, heirloom bed quilt. ~ Corey

Materials

Yardage is based on 42"-wide fabric.

2⅞ yards of off-white solid for blocks

⅜ yard of red solid for blocks

⅞ yard of green solid for appliqués

½ yard of red-and-green diagonal stripe for binding*

3½ yards of fabric for backing

61" × 61" piece of batting

1¾ yards of 17"-wide paper-backed fusible web

*If the stripe you're using is not printed on the diagonal but you want the same look, cut your binding strips on the bias. Increase yardage to ⅝ yard for fewer strips to piece together.

Cutting

All measurements include ¼" seam allowances.

From the off-white solid, cut:

12 strips, 6½" × 42"; crosscut into:
    18 rectangles, 6½" × 18½"
    18 squares, 6½" × 6½"
6 strips, 2" × 42"; crosscut into:
    36 rectangles, 2" × 3½"
    36 squares, 2" × 2"

From the red solid, cut:

1 strip, 3½" × 42"; crosscut into 9 squares, 3½" × 3½"
4 strips, 2" × 42"; crosscut into 72 squares, 2" × 2"

From the red-and-green stripe, cut:

6 strips, 2½" × 42"

Making the Pieced Blocks

Press all seam allowances as indicated by the arrows.

1. Draw a diagonal line from corner to corner on the wrong side of each red 2" square. Align a marked red 2" square with one end of an off-white 2" × 3½" rectangle, right sides together and orienting the line as shown. Sew on the line. Trim the seam allowances to ¼" and press. Repeat to add a second marked square to the other end of the rectangle, orienting the line as shown, to make a star-point unit that measures 2" × 3½", including seam allowances. Make 36 units.

Make 36 units,
2" × 3½".

By Corey Yoder; machine quilted by Rebecca Silbaugh

QUILT SIZE: 54½" × 54½" **BLOCK SIZE:** 18" × 18"

2. Lay out four off-white 2" squares, four star-point units, and one red 3½" square in three rows. Sew together the pieces in each row. Join the rows to make a star unit that measures 6½" square, including seam allowances. Make nine star units.

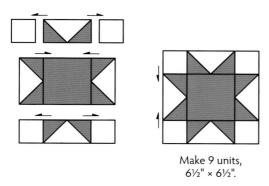

Make 9 units,
6½" × 6½".

3. Sew off-white 6½" squares to opposite edges of a star unit. Add off-white 6½" × 18½" rectangles to the remaining edges to make a block that measures 18½" square, including seam allowances. Make nine blocks.

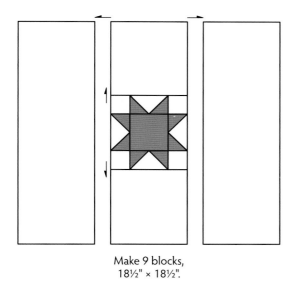

Make 9 blocks,
18½" × 18½".

Adding the Appliqués

Corey used fusible appliqué, and the instructions that follow reflect that method. For more information on a variety of appliqué techniques, you can go to ShopMartingale.com/HowtoQuilt.

1. Using the patterns on page 66, prepare 140 petals and 20 stems for appliqué by tracing the patterns onto the paper side of fusible web. Adhere the fusible to the wrong side of the appliqué fabric and cut out

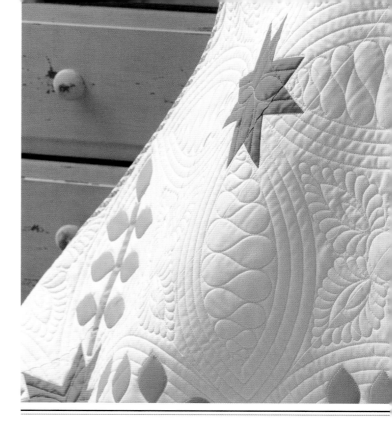

on the drawn lines. For faster and more accurate tracing, make a plastic template for each appliqué shape and draw around the shape onto fusible web.

2. Fold a pieced block in half twice diagonally and crease to create placement lines; unfold. Position one stem and seven petals in each quadrant of the block, placing the stem on the crease line. Fuse in place following the manufacturer's instructions. Blanket-stitch around each appliqué by hand or machine. Make five appliquéd blocks.

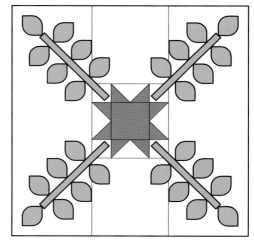

Make 5 appliquéd blocks.

Assembling the Quilt Top

1. Lay out the blocks in three rows of three blocks each, alternating the appliquéd and pieced blocks. Rotate the blocks so that you avoid intersecting seams on the sides of the blocks.

2. Sew the blocks together in each row. Join the rows to complete the quilt top, which should measure 54½" square.

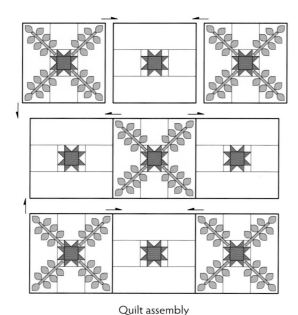

Quilt assembly

Finishing the Quilt

For more details on any finishing steps, visit ShopMartingale.com/HowtoQuilt for free downloadable information.

1. Layer the backing, batting, and quilt top; baste the layers together.

2. Quilt by hand or machine. The quilt shown is machine quilted with an echoing orange peel design around the appliqués in each block. The pieced blocks feature the same orange peel motif filled in with a ribbon candy design. Each off-white area between the orange peel sections is filled with feathers. Each red star is quilted with a smaller orange peel and straight lines parallel to the seams of the star points.

3. Use the striped 2½"-wide strips to make binding, and then attach the binding to the quilt.

Appliqué patterns do not include seam allowances.

Petal
Cut 140 from green solid.

Stem
Cut 20 from green solid.

HERITAGE MOUNTAIN

BY SHERYL JOHNSON

Most of my quilts are scrappy, so you may be surprised that my red-and-green quilt is controlled. I love the vintage look—it resembles a quilt that our grandmothers may have made from calicoes. ~Sheryl

Materials

Yardage is based on 42"-wide fabric.

1½ yards of red print #1 for blocks and sashing

1 yard of red print #2 for outer border

1⅔ yards of green print #1 for blocks and binding

1¼ yards of green print #2 for blocks, sashing squares, and inner border

3⅛ yards of light print for blocks and borders

3⅔ yards of fabric for backing

65" × 80" piece of batting

Cutting

All measurements include ¼" seam allowances.

From red print #1, cut:

6 strips, 3¼" × 42"; crosscut into 72 squares, 3¼" × 3¼". Cut *24* of the squares in half diagonally to make 48 triangles.

2 strips, 13¼" × 42"; crosscut into 31 strips, 2½" × 13¼"

From red print #2, cut:

7 strips, 4½" × 42"

From green print #1, cut:

20 strips, 1¾" × 42"; crosscut into 432 squares, 1¾" × 1¾"

7 strips, 2½" × 42"

From green print #2, cut:

8 strips, 3" × 42"; crosscut into 100 squares, 3" × 3"

2 strips, 2½" × 42"; crosscut into:

    2 rectangles, 2½" × 2¾"

    24 squares, 2½" × 2½"

    2 rectangles, 1½" × 2½"

1 strip, 2" × 42"; crosscut into 12 squares, 2" × 2"

3 strips, 1⅞" × 42"; crosscut into 48 squares, 1⅞" × 1⅞"

From the light print cut:

2 strips, 5¾" × 42"; crosscut into 12 squares, 5¾" × 5¾". Cut into quarters diagonally to make 48 *side* triangles.

4 strips, 5½" × 42"; crosscut into 24 squares, 5½" × 5½". Cut in half diagonally to make 48 *corner* triangles.

4 strips, 3¼" × 42"; crosscut into 48 squares, 3¼" × 3¼"

5 strips, 3" × 42"; crosscut into 64 squares, 3" × 3

20 strips, 1¾" × 42"; crosscut into 432 squares, 1¾" × 1¾"

6 strips, 1¼" × 42"; crosscut into 192 squares, 1¼" × 1¼"

Making the Half-Square-Triangle Units

Press all seam allowances as indicated by the arrows.

1. Draw a diagonal line from corner to corner on the wrong side of each light 1¾" square, 3¼" square, and 52 of the 3" squares.

2. Layer a marked 1¾" square on a green 1¾" square, right sides together. Stitch a scant ¼" from both sides of the marked line. Cut on the line to make two half-square-triangle units. Trim the units to 1¼" square. Make 864 half-square-triangle units for the blocks.

Make 864 units.

3. Using marked light 3¼" squares and the red 3¼" squares, make 96 half-square-triangle units for the blocks. Trim each to 2¾" square.

Make 96 units.

4. Using marked light 3" squares and the green 3" squares, make 104 half-square-triangle units for the borders. Trim each to 2½" square.

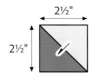

Make 104 units.

Making the Block Centers

1. Draw a diagonal line on the wrong side of each green 1⅞" square. Place marked green squares on opposite corners of a light 3" square. Stitch a scant ¼" from each side of the drawn line. Cut apart on the drawn line. Place a marked green square on one of the units and stitch a scant ¼" from each side of

the drawn line. Cut along the drawn line to make two star-point units. Repeat to make two additional star-point units. Trim each star-point unit to 1¼" × 2". Repeat to make 48 units.

Make 48 units.

2. Join four light 1¼" squares, four star-point units, and one green 2" square in three rows as shown. Join the rows to make a star unit. Repeat to make 12 star units, each 3½" square, including seam allowances.

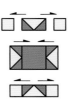

Make 12 units, 3½" × 3½".

3. Fold a red triangle in half and crease it to mark the center of the long side. Pin and sew it to one side of a star unit, lining up the crease with the center of the star unit. Repeat on the opposite side. Then add triangles to the remaining sides of the star

By Sheryl Johnson; machine quilted by Peggy Gulserian

QUILT SIZE: 58¾" × 73½" ❧ **BLOCK SIZE:** 12¾" × 12¾"

unit. Trim the unit to 5" square, keeping the star centered. Make 12 bordered star units.

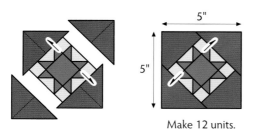

Make 12 units.

4. Sew together two light 1¼" squares and six light/green 1¼" half-square-triangle units as shown. Make 24 top/bottom rows, each 1¼" × 6½", including seam allowances.

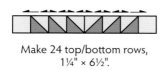

Make 24 top/bottom rows,
1¼" × 6½".

5. In the same manner, join six light/green 1¼" half-square-triangle units to make a side row. Make 24 side rows, each 1¼" × 5", including seam allowances.

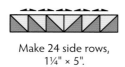

Make 24 side rows,
1¼" × 5".

6. Sew side rows to opposite edges of a bordered star unit. Add top/bottom rows to the remaining edges to complete the block center. Make sure the green edges of the rows are adjacent to the star unit. The block center should be 6½" square, including seam allowances. Make 12.

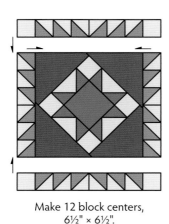

Make 12 block centers,
6½" × 6½".

Making the Blocks

1. Sew together three light/green 1¼" half-square-triangle units in a row. Sew the row to a light/red 2¾" half-square-triangle unit as shown. Join one light 1¼" square and three half-square-triangle units in a row; sew this row to the remaining red edge of the unit. Make 96 Delectable Mountain block units, each 3½" square, including seam allowances.

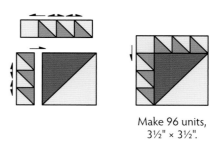

Make 96 units,
3½" × 3½".

2. Join two Delectable Mountain units to make a pair that measures 3½" × 6½". Make 48 pairs.

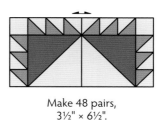

Make 48 pairs,
3½" × 6½".

3. Lay out one block center, four Delectable Mountain pairs, four light 5¾" side triangles, and four light 5½" corner triangles in diagonal rows as shown. Sew the block center and Delectable Mountain pairs together into rows. Join the rows, matching the seam intersections. Add the corner triangles last. Trim the block to 13¼" square. Make 12 blocks.

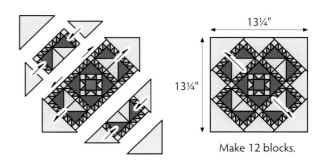

Make 12 blocks.

4. Draw a diagonal line from corner to corner on the wrong side of the green 3" squares. Align a marked square on each corner of a block, right side down and edges aligned. Sew the two together along the marked diagonal line. Trim the excess corner fabric, leaving a ¼" seam allowance. Repeat for each block.

Adding the corners

Assembling the Quilt

1. Referring to the quilt assembly diagram below, arrange the blocks in four rows of three blocks each. Add the red 2½" × 13¼" sashing strips and green 2½" sashing squares.

2. Sew the blocks and sashing pieces together in each row, and then join the rows. The quilt center should be 46¾" × 61½", including seam allowances.

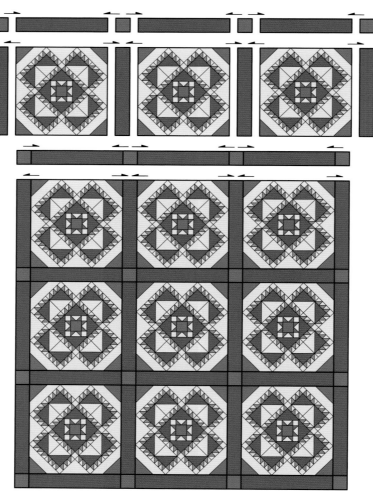

Quilt assembly

3. Sew together 22 of the light/green 2½" half-square-triangle units and one green 2½" × 2¾" rectangle as shown to make an inner border that measures 2½" × 46¾", including seam allowances. Make two.

Make 2 top/bottom borders,
2½" × 46¾".

4. Join two green 2½" squares, 30 light/green 2½" half-square-triangle units, and one green 1½" × 2½" rectangle as shown to make a side inner border that measures 2½" × 65½", including seam allowances. Make two.

Make 2 side borders,
2½" × 65½".

5. Sew the top/bottom inner borders to the top and bottom edges of the quilt center. Sew the side inner borders to the remaining edges. Make sure the green edges of the borders are adjacent to the quilt center.

6. Join the red 4½" × 42" strips end to end and press the seam allowances open. Trim the pieced length into two 73½"-long outer-border strips and two 50¾"-long outer-border strips. Sew the shorter strips to top and bottom edges of the quilt center. Sew the

longer strips to the remaining edges to complete the quilt top, which should measure 58¾" × 73½".

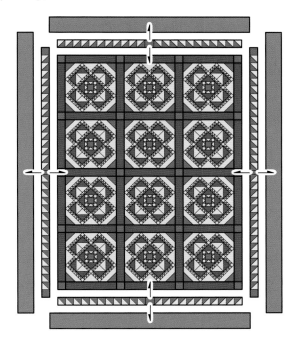

Adding the borders

Finishing the Quilt

For more details on any finishing steps, visit ShopMartingale.com/HowtoQuilt for free downloadable information.

1. Layer the backing, batting, and quilt top; baste the layers together.

2. Quilt by hand or machine. The quilt shown is machine quilted in an allover medium-size meander.

3. Use the green 2½"-wide strips to make binding, and then attach the binding to the quilt.

PRIMROSE HOLLY

BY LISA BONGEAN

Indulge your love of wool and soft textures with this lovely four-block appliqué quilt, reminiscent of the classic quilts popular from the mid- to late-nineteenth century. Coincidentally, the pairing of red and green was the most commonly used color combination of that same period. ~Lisa

Materials

Yardage is based on 42"-wide fabric. Wool sizes are for wool that has already been felted.

5¾ yards of off-white solid flannel for background, border, and binding

1 rectangle, 10" × 11", of green wool for stems

4 rectangles, 12" × 18" *each,* of assorted green wools for leaves and flowers

5 squares, 12" × 12" *each,* of assorted red wools for circles and flowers

1 square, 5" × 5", of ivory wool for flowers

4 yards of fabric for backing

71" × 71" piece of batting

4¼ yards of 12"-wide Lite Steam-a-Seam 2 paper-backed fusible web

Valdani #8 pearl cotton in the following colors: variegated red, green, and ivory

Chenille needle, size 22

Cutting

All measurements include ¼" seam allowances.

From the *lengthwise* grain of the off-white flannel, cut:
2 strips, 8½" × 64½"
2 strips, 8½" × 48½"

From the *remaining* off-white flannel, cut:
4 squares, 26" × 26"
7 strips, 2½" × 42"

Preparing the Stems

1. Cut a 9" × 10" piece of fusible web. Remove the paper backing to expose the tacky side of the fusible web. Center the web on the green wool 10" × 11" rectangle. Fuse in place with a dry iron.

2. Using a rotary cutter, cut 16 stems, ½" × 9½", from the fused green wool. Do not remove the remaining paper backing yet.

By Lisa Bongean; machine quilted by Linda Hrcka

QUILT SIZE: 64½" × 64½" ❧ **BLOCK SIZE:** 24" × 24"

Preparing the Wool Appliqués

1. Place a green wool 12" × 18" rectangle on the gridded side of the fusible web. Lightly mark the perimeter of the wool. Repeat to loosely trace all four rectangles of green wool, the five red wool squares, and the ivory wool square.

2. Trace the appliqué shapes using the patterns on page 79 as listed onto the fusible web *within* the perimeter lines of each section you've drawn. This makes the most efficient use of your fusible web, wool, and time. There's no need to leave space between the drawn shapes because there's no seam allowance on these pieces.

- Trace 20 small leaves, four large leaves, and one small flower on *each* 12" × 18" rectangle.
- Trace 58 circles on *each* 12" square (two circles will be extra). Trace one large flower on four of the squares.
- Trace four medium flowers on the 5" square.

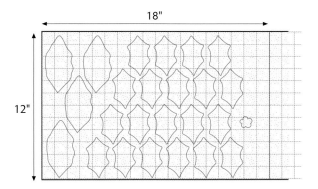

3. Roughly cut out each section of fusible web (the *entire group* of shapes for each wool piece) about ⅛" from the perimeter of the traced pieces.

4. Carefully peel off the paper backing to expose the tacky side of the fusible web. Make sure the fusible layer stays with the gridded paper side you traced on. Position each section of web on the wrong side of the corresponding wool piece.

5. With a dry iron, press the fusible web onto the wool to adhere it. Allow the wool to cool and then cut out all of the individual shapes, cutting on or just inside the drawn lines. Do not remove the remaining paper backing yet.

Appliquéing the Blocks

1. Fold each white 26" square in half diagonally in each direction; crease lightly to mark placement lines.

2. Referring to the appliqué placement diagram, position one green stem, 18 red circles, and four small green leaves along the diagonal in each quadrant of the square; remove the backing paper right before you place each piece. In the center of the block, position four large green leaves, four small green leaves, one large red flower, one medium ivory flower, and one small green flower.

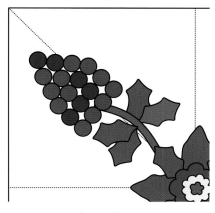

Appliqué placement

3. Fuse all of the appliqués in place using steam and the highest wool setting. Blanket-stitch around each appliqué piece and add stem-stitched details inside each leaf. Stitch seven French knots in the center of the small green flower. (Refer to the illustrations for blanket stitch, French knots, and stem stitch on page 78.) Make four appliquéd blocks and trim each to 24½" square, keeping the designs centered.

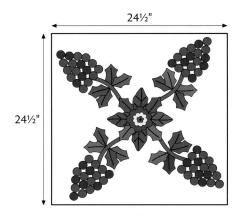

Make 4 blocks.

Finishing the Quilt

For more details on any finishing steps, visit ShopMartingale.com/HowtoQuilt for free downloadable information.

1. Layer the backing, batting, and quilt top; baste the layers together.

2. Quilt by hand or machine. The quilt shown is machine quilted with a circle and curved grid in each block. The background is meander quilted and the border features a feathered cable.

3. Use the off-white flannel 2½"-wide strips to make binding, and then attach the binding to the quilt.

Assembling the Quilt

Press all seam allowances as indicated by the arrows.

1. Sew together the blocks in two rows of two blocks each. Join the rows. The quilt center should be 48½" square, including seam allowances.

2. Sew the off-white 8½" × 48½" strips to opposite sides of the quilt center. Add the white 8½" × 64½" strips to the top and bottom to complete the quilt top. It should measure 64½" square.

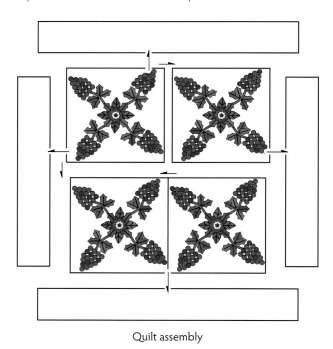

Quilt assembly

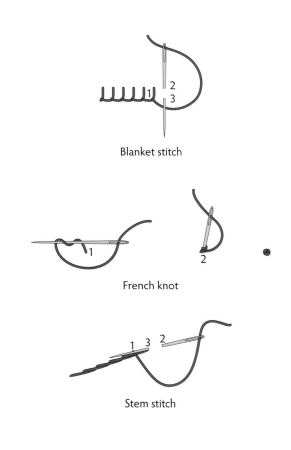

Blanket stitch

French knot

Stem stitch

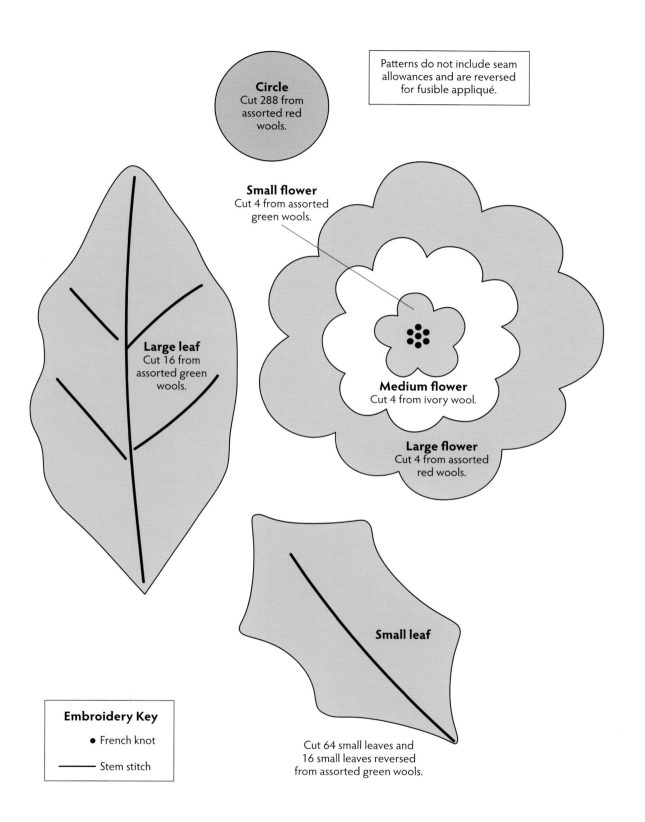

Circle
Cut 288 from
assorted red
wools.

Patterns do not include seam
allowances and are reversed
for fusible appliqué.

Small flower
Cut 4 from assorted
green wools.

Large leaf
Cut 16 from
assorted green
wools.

Medium flower
Cut 4 from ivory wool.

Large flower
Cut 4 from assorted
red wools.

Small leaf

Cut 64 small leaves and
16 small leaves reversed
from assorted green wools.

Embroidery Key

● French knot

— Stem stitch

Home Sweet Home

BY PAM BUDA

You can definitely say that I'm detail oriented—I just love adding details to my quilts. For my red-and-green beauty, I've incorporated pieced setting blocks and pieced borders. All of the elements involve easy piecing but create a quilt with a beautifully complex look. ~Pam

Materials

Yardage is based on 42"-wide fabric.

4½ yards of cream print for blocks and borders

⅓ yard *each* of 8 assorted red prints for blocks and borders

⅓ yard *each* of 8 assorted green prints for blocks and borders

½ yard of green print #1 for border 5

⅞ yard of red print for border 6

⅝ yard of green print #2 for binding

3⅝ yards of fabric for backing

64" × 77" piece of batting

Cutting

All measurements include ¼" seam allowances. Keep like fabrics together and label the pieces by size as you cut.

From the cream print, cut:

2 strips, 6½" × 42"; crosscut into 14 rectangles, 5½" × 6½"

6 strips, 4½" × 42"; crosscut into:
   17 squares, 4½" × 4½"
   82 rectangles, 1½" × 4½"

28 strips, 2¼" × 42"; crosscut into 472 squares, 2¼" × 2¼"

7 strips, 1⅞" × 42" crosscut into 132 squares, 1⅞" × 1⅞". Cut in half diagonally to make 264 triangles.

17 strips, 1½" × 42"; crosscut *6* of the strips into 140 squares, 1½" × 1½"

From *each* of the assorted red prints, cut:

4 squares, 2⅞" × 2⅞"; cut in half diagonally to make 8 triangles (64 total)

29 squares, 2¼" × 2¼" (232 total)

14 squares, 1½" × 1½" (112 total)

Continued on page 83

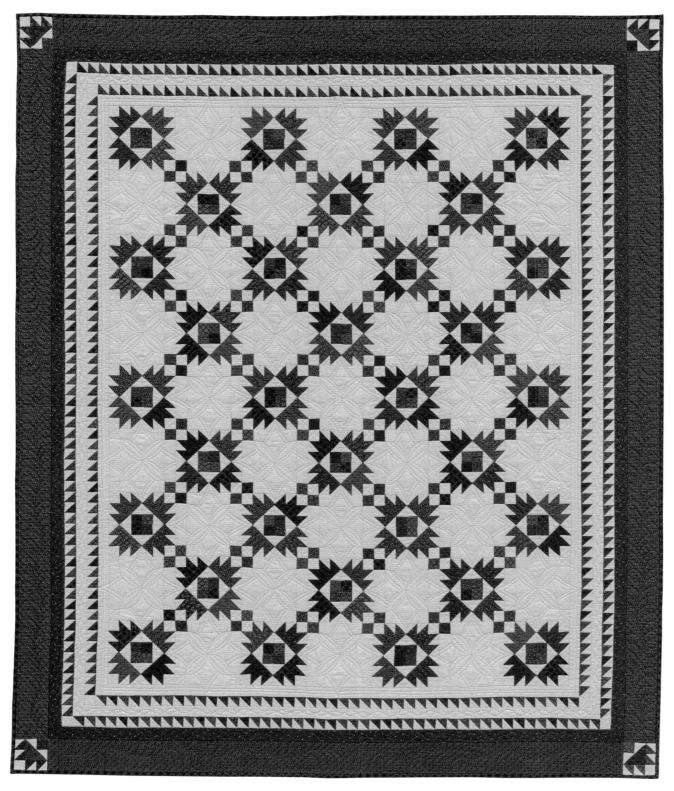

By Pam Buda; pieced by Pam Buda and Debbie McClarence; machine quilted by Valerie Krueger

QUILT SIZE: 59" × 71" **BLOCK SIZE:** 6" × 6"

Continued from page 80

From *each of 2* of the assorted red prints, cut:

1 square, 2⅞" × 2⅞"; cut in half diagonally to make
    2 triangles (4 total)

From *each* of the assorted green prints, cut:

4 squares, 2⅞"; cut in half diagonally to make
    8 triangles (64 total)
29 squares, 2¼" × 2¼" (232 total)
14 squares, 1½" × 1½" (112 total)

From *the remainder* of the assorted green prints, cut:

4 *matching sets* of:
    2 squares, 2¼" × 2¼" (8 total)
    1 square, 1½" × 1½" (4 total)

From green print #1, cut:

6 strips, 1¾" × 42"

From the red print for border 6, cut:

7 strips, 3½" × 42"

From green print #2, cut:

7 strips, 2¼" × 42"

Making the Four Crowns Blocks

Press all seam allowances as indicated by the arrows.

1. Choose two red 2¼" squares and a red 2⅞" triangle—all matching—for one red crown unit.

2. Draw a diagonal line on the wrong side of two cream 2¼" squares. Align right sides together with each red 2¼" square and sew ¼" from each side of the drawn line. Cut apart on the line. Make four half-square-triangle units. Trim to 1½" square.

Make 4 units.

3. Sew two cream 1⅞" triangles to a green 1½" square to make a pieced triangle unit.

Make 1 unit.

4. Sew the red 2⅞" triangle to the pieced triangle unit to make a shaded four-patch unit that measures 2½" square, including seam allowances.

Make 1 unit,
2½" × 2½".

✎ Easy Trim ✎

Pam used Deb Tucker's Tucker Trimmer 1 ruler to make the shaded four-patch units without cutting *any* triangles. Using the ruler, the pieces are cut larger than needed, allowing you to trim the unit to the perfect size. The tool is optional, but a time-saver.

5. Arrange the four half-square-triangle units, the shaded four-patch unit, and one cream 1½" square as shown. Sew the half-square-triangle units into two pairs and then sew the units together in rows. Sew the rows together to make a red crown unit that measures 3½" square, including seam allowances. Make 64 red crown units.

Make 64 units,
3½" × 3½".

6. Repeat steps 1–5, swapping green pieces for red and vice versa. Press the seam allowances of the half-square-triangle units toward the green in step 2. Make 64 green crown units.

Make 64 units,
3½" × 3½".

7. Arrange two red and two green crown units as shown. Sew together into rows and then join the rows to complete a Four Crowns block that measures 6½" square, including seam allowances. Make a total of 32 blocks.

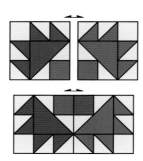 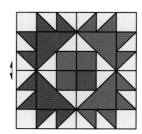

Make 32 blocks,
6½" × 6½".

Making the Alternate Blocks

1. Sew two different-red 1½" squares to the ends of a cream 1½" × 4½" rectangle to make a unit that measures 1½" × 6½", including seam allowances. Repeat with two different-green 1½" squares. Make a total of 21 of each.

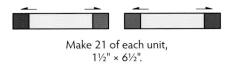

Make 21 of each unit,
1½" × 6½".

2. Sew a green 1½" square to the left side of a cream 1½" × 4½" rectangle and a red 1½" square to the right side to make a unit that measures 1½" × 6½", including seam allowances. Make a total of six units.

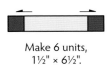

Make 6 units,
1½" × 6½".

3. Sew cream 1½" × 4½" rectangles to the top and bottom of a cream 4½" square to make a unit that measures 4½" × 6½", including seam allowances. Make 17 units.

Make 17 units,
4½" × 6½".

4. Sew a red step 1 unit to the right side of a unit from step 3 and sew a green step 1 unit to the left side to make an alternate block for the center of the quilt. It should measure 6½" square, including seam allowances. Make a total of 17 blocks.

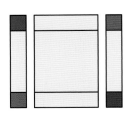 

Make 17 blocks,
6½" × 6½".

5. Sew the units from steps 1 and 2 to the cream 5½" × 6½" rectangles as shown to make 14 alternate blocks for the sides, top, and bottom of the quilt. They should measure 6½" square, including seam allowances.

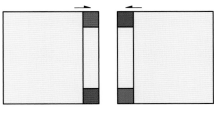

Make 4 of each block,
6½" × 6½".

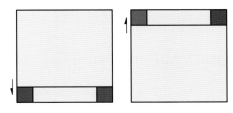

Make 3 of each block,
6½" × 6½".

❧ Measure of Success ❧

Measuring units at each step of the piecing process is time well spent. Especially when making a quilt with a pieced border! Measuring each unit and block as it's made means catching errors when seams are small and knowing that your blocks are the correct size. It means quilt centers, plain borders, and pieced borders fit!

Assembling the Quilt Center

Arrange the blocks in nine rows of seven blocks each, alternating the blocks as shown in the quilt assembly diagram below. Make sure the alternate blocks are positioned and oriented correctly. Sew the blocks together into rows and then join the rows. The quilt center should measure 42½" × 54½", including seam allowances.

Making the Border Units

1. Draw a diagonal line on the wrong side of 208 cream 2¼" squares. Place a marked square right sides together with a red or green 2¼" square and sew ¼" on each side of the drawn line. Cut apart on the line to make a half-square-triangle unit. Press and trim to 1½" square. Make 208 red and 208 green units.

Make 208 of each unit.

2. Repeat step 1, drawing the diagonal line on the wrong side of eight cream 2¼" squares. Place a marked square right sides together with *four matching sets of two* green 2¼" squares. Make a total of 16 half-square-triangle units for the outer-border corner blocks.

Make 16 units.

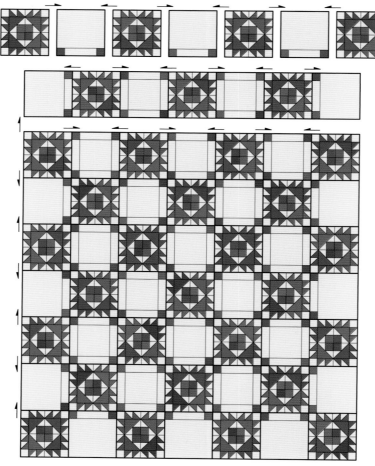

Quilt assembly

3. Sew two cream 1⅞" triangles to a green 1½" square to make a pieced triangle. Make four units.

Make 4 units.

4. Sew a red 2⅞" triangle to a pieced triangle to make a shaded four-patch unit that measures 2½" square, including seam allowances. Make a total of four units, two each of two different red prints.

Make 4 units,
2½" × 2½".

5. Arrange four green half-square-triangle units from step 2, one unit from step 4, and a cream 1½" square as shown. Sew the half-square-triangle units into two pairs and sew the units into rows. Join the rows to make a corner block that measures 3½" square, including seam allowances. Make four blocks.

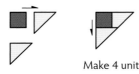

Make 4 blocks,
3½" × 3½".

Adding the Borders

It's always best to measure your quilt from top to bottom before adding side borders. Make sure the side borders are the correct length. Then, measure your quilt from side to side, including the just-added side borders. Be sure that the top and bottom borders are the correct length. Doing this for each of the borders will ensure that your quilt top will be straight and even when completed.

1. Join five cream 1½"-wide strips end to end. Cut two strips, 1½" × 54½", for the sides and two strips, 1½" × 44½", for the top and bottom. Sew the longer borders to sides of the quilt center and then the shorter borders to the top and bottom. Press seam allowances toward the cream border. The quilt center should measure 44½" × 56½", including seam allowances.

2. Join 56 half-square-triangle units, beginning with a green print and alternating with red. Make two borders measuring 1½" × 56½", including seam allowances. Join 44 units, beginning with a green print and alternating with red. Add a cream 1½" square to each end. Make two borders for the top and bottom that measure 1½" × 46½", including seam allowances.

Make 2 borders,
1½" × 56½".

Make 2 borders,
1½" × 46½".

3. Sew a pieced border to each side of the quilt center and then sew the pieced borders to the top and bottom. Press seam allowances toward the cream border. The quilt center should measure 46½" × 58½", including seam allowances.

4. Join six cream 1½"-wide strips end to end. Cut two strips, 1½" × 58½", for the sides and two strips, 1½" × 48½", for the top and bottom. Sew the longer borders to sides of the quilt center and then the shorter borders to the top and bottom. Press seam allowances toward the cream border. The quilt center should measure 48½" × 60½", including seam allowances.

5. Join 60 half-square-triangle units, beginning with a green print and alternating with red. Make two pieced borders for the sides measuring 1½" × 60½", including seam allowances. Sew 48 units together, beginning with a green print and alternating with red. Add a cream 1½" square to each end. Make two pieced borders for the top and bottom that measure 1½" × 50½", including seam allowances.

Make 2 borders,
1½" × 60½".

Make 2 borders,
1½" × 50½".

6. Sew a pieced border to each side of the quilt center and then sew the pieced borders to the top and bottom. The quilt center should measure 50½" × 62½", including seam allowances.

7. Join the six green 1¾"-wide strips end to end. Cut two strips, 1¾" × 62½", for the sides and two strips, 1¾" × 53", for the top and bottom. Sew the longer borders to sides of the quilt center and then the shorter borders to the top and bottom. The quilt center should measure 53" × 65", including seam allowances.

8. Join the seven red 3½"-wide strips end to end. Cut two strips, 3½" × 65", for the sides and two strips, 3½" × 53", for the top and bottom. Add a corner block to each end of the 3½" × 53" strips for the top and bottom borders, referring to the diagram to make sure the blocks are oriented correctly.

9. Sew the side borders to the sides of the quilt center and then add the top and bottom borders. The quilt top should measure 59" × 71".

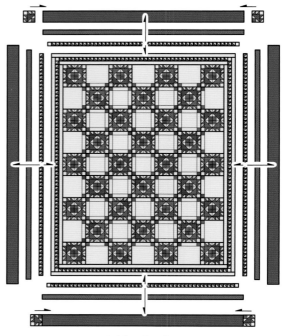

Adding borders

Finishing the Quilt

For more details on any finishing steps, visit ShopMartingale.com/HowtoQuilt for free downloadable information.

1. Layer the backing, batting, and quilt top; baste the layers together.

2. Quilt by hand or machine. The quilt shown is machine quilted with petals and arcs in the alternate blocks and a loop design in the crown units. A curved feathered vine fills the outer border.

3. Use the green 2¼"-wide strips to make binding, and then attach the binding to the quilt.

Tudor Rose

BY KAREN STYLES

I've always had a fascination with red-and-green quilts. The striking contrast of the two colors against a light background is very dynamic. I've also wanted to make a large appliqué piece for some time. Being asked to design a quilt for this book gave me the perfect opportunity. ~Karen

Materials

Yardage is based on 42"-wide fabric. Fat eighths measure 9" × 21".

4⅜ yards of cream solid for appliqué backgrounds and border

2¾ yards of green check for appliqués, stems, and bias binding

⅔ yard of red print for appliqués

⅓ yard of red pinstripe for appliqués

1 fat eighth of gold solid for appliqués

3¾ yards of fabric for backing

67" × 67" piece of batting

Water-soluble stabilizer for preparing the appliqués (optional)*

Water-soluble fabric glue stick or basting glue

Ceramic marking pencil

*Karen used Polyfuse from Matilda's Own, an iron-on stabilizer. A similar product is Floriani Stitch N Wash fusible stabilizer from RNK Distributing.

Cutting

All measurements include ¼" seam allowances.

From the *lengthwise* grain of the cream solid, cut:
1 piece, 42" × 60½"; from this piece, cut:
    2 strips, 10½" × 60½"
    1 strip, 10½" × 40½"
1 piece, 42" × 90"; from this piece, cut:
    4 squares, 22" × 22"
    1 strip, 10½" × 40½"

From the green check, cut:
255" *total* of 2½"-wide bias strips
8 bias strips, 1½" × 17"
8 bias strips, 1½" × 11"
4 bias strips, 2¼" × 5¾"
4 bias strips, 2¼" × 4½"
Save all remaining fabric for appliqués.

From the red print, cut *on the bias*:
8 strips, ¾" × 3½"
Save all remaining fabric for appliqués.

Preparing the Appliqués

Karen used a water-soluble stabilizer to prepare appliqué shapes, but you could substitute freezer paper if you prefer. Remove it either just before appliquéing or after by carefully cutting a slit in the background fabric. For more information on appliqué techniques, go to ShopMartingale.com/HowtoQuilt.

1. Using the patterns on pages 96 and 97, trace the shapes the number of times specified onto the dull side of the stabilizer using a ceramic pencil. Cut out carefully and smoothly on the drawn lines to make templates.

2. Press the shiny side of each paper template onto the wrong side of the indicated fabric with an iron, leaving at least ½" between shapes. Cut out each fabric shape, leaving a scant ¼" seam allowance around each piece.

3. Using a fabric glue stick or basting glue, run a line of glue along the edge of the fabric. Finger-press the fabric seam allowances over the edges of the paper templates. Gently gather the curves as you go to form smooth curved edges. Do not glue or turn under any sections that will be placed under other sections of appliqué; these are marked in blue on the patterns.

Making the Blocks

1. Fold each cream 22" square in half and make a gentle crease. Fold the square the other direction and make another crease. Then fold diagonally in both directions to make two additional creases. Each background square will now have eight creases radiating from the center; these will be used as the placement locations for the large green flower bases.

2. Using the creased placement lines as a guide and referring to the appliqué placement diagram, position eight green large flower bases on a block, placing the bottom of the stems 2½" from the center point. Pin onto the background square and position a red pinstripe large flower bottom and red print

large flower top under each base. Lay the green leaves in place under the stem, two leaves per stem, keeping an even and consistent placement. Placing the leaves under the vine eliminates the need for appliquéing narrow points. When you're happy with the placement, thread baste or glue baste in place.

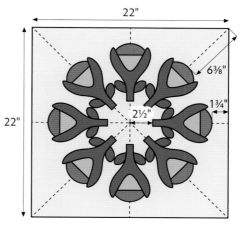

Appliqué placement

3. Appliqué the shapes to the background. Start with the leaves, the red print flower tops, and the red pinstripe section, and finish with the green check stems. Repeat to make four blocks.

4. To create the center flower sections, arrange and baste eight red print clam-shape petals and eight red pinstripe triangular petals in a circle, using the large red print circle as a guide. Appliqué the petals together to form a circular chain. Place a large red print circle and gold small circle atop the joined petals, covering their raw edges; glue baste in place. Appliqué the circles in place to make a center flower. Make five flowers.

Appliqué placement.
Make 5 flowers.

5. Center a flower on each block and appliqué onto the background square. (The fifth flower is for the center of the quilt and will be added after the blocks

By Karen Styles

QUILT SIZE: 60½" × 60½" ❧ **BLOCK SIZE:** 20" × 20"

are joined.) Press each block and trim to 20½" square, including seam allowances.

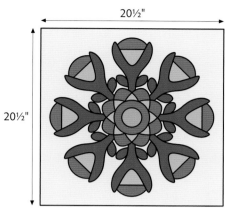

20½"

20½"

Make 4 blocks.

Assembling the Quilt

Press all seam allowances as indicated by the arrows.

1. Sew together four blocks in two rows. Join the rows to make the quilt center, which should be 40½" square, including seam allowances.

2. Appliqué the remaining center flower, centering it over the seam intersection of the four blocks.

3. Sew the cream 10½" × 40½" strips to the side edges of the quilt center. Add the cream 10½" × 60½" strips to the top and bottom. The quilt top should now be 60½" square.

Preparing the Bias Strips and Appliqués

1. Fold over one-third of the width of a green 1½" × 17" bias strip and press with a dry iron. Gently fold over the remaining third by hand and tack along the length with dots of basting glue or a fabric glue stick. Make eight green vines, ½" × 17".

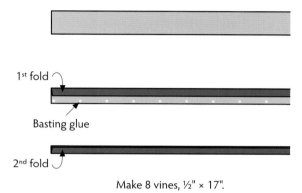

1st fold

Basting glue

2nd fold

Make 8 vines, ½" × 17".

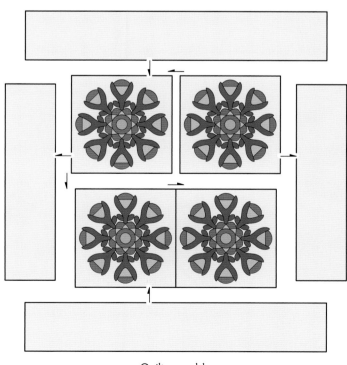

Quilt assembly

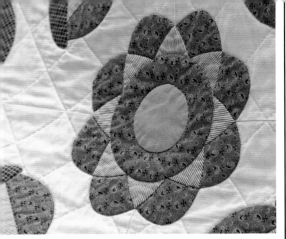

2. Prepare the remaining bias strips in the same manner to make the following:

- 8 green vines, ½" × 11"
- 4 green stems, ¾" × 5¾"
- 4 green stems, ¾" × 4½"
- 8 red strips, ¼" × 3½"

3. Appliqué a vase lip and red bias strip to each vase. Appliqué the tulip flower base, tulip center, and tulip petals together to create the flower unit. Appliqué the bud and small flower base together. Make eight vase units, eight tulip units, and 40 bud units.

Make 8 of each unit.   Make 40 units.

Appliquéing the Border

1. Referring to the appliqué placement guide, mark the centers of the side borders by folding them in half. Lightly mark the placement of the vine and leaves with a sharp pencil on both sides.

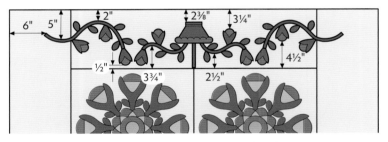

Appliqué placement guide, side borders

2. Referring to the appliqué placement guide, lightly mark the placement of the vine and leaves on the top and bottom borders.

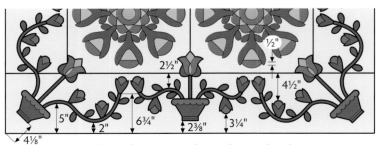

Appliqué placement guide, top/bottom borders

3. Pin the vines and stems in place using a "hurdle" technique. Refer to "Pin-Basting Bias Vines and Stems" below.

Pin-Basting
❧ Bias Vines and Stems ❧

Position a vine on the background fabric where marked. Insert a pin into the background, perpendicular to the vine and about ¼" away from the vine. Bring the pin up again, catching about ⅛" of the background fabric only. Do not pin through the vine. Take the pin over the vine and insert it into the background just along the edge of the vine; come up about ⅛" away on the other side of the vine, creating the "hurdle." You'll need to use many pins for each bias vine or stem. This allows the bias vine to be manipulated freely as you stitch, making perfect curves for vines and stems. Remove the pins as you stitch along the edge. Because the bias strips have been tacked along the length, they won't undo or flip open before you finish stitching.

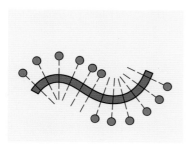

4. Arrange the leaves in position under the vine and pin in place. Check the placement of the leaves and glue baste or thread baste in place.

5. Using thread that matches the vine, appliqué the vine and leaves.

6. Appliqué the buds on top of the vines.

7. Appliqué the green ¾" × 5¾" stems in the border corners and stitch a tulip at the top. Appliqué the green ¾" × 4½" stems in the center of the side borders and stitch a tulip to the top of each.

8. Appliqué the vase units, making sure the vases are centered over the vines and stems.

9. Continue appliquéing the units in place along the borders until you have worked your way around the entire quilt.

Appliqué placement guide

Finishing the Quilt

For more details on any finishing steps, visit ShopMartingale.com/HowtoQuilt for free downloadable information.

1. Layer the backing, batting, and quilt top; baste the layers together.

2. Quilt by hand or machine. The quilt shown is machine quilted with a traditional diagonal crosshatch grid in the background.

3. Use the green check 2½"-wide bias strips to make binding, and then attach the binding to the quilt.

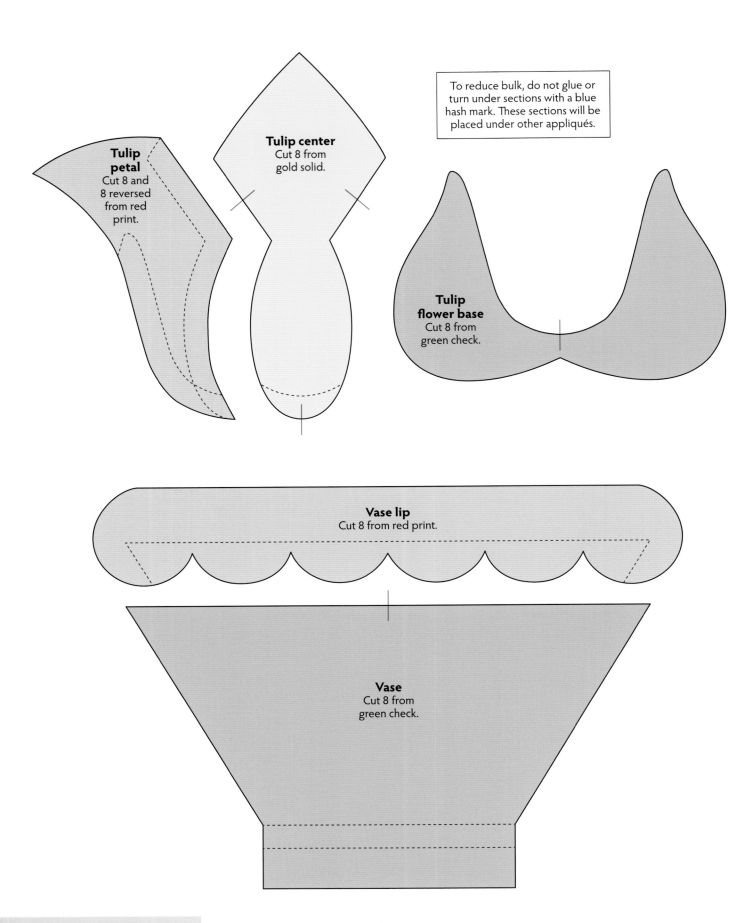

Tulip petal
Cut 8 and 8 reversed from red print.

Tulip center
Cut 8 from gold solid.

To reduce bulk, do not glue or turn under sections with a blue hash mark. These sections will be placed under other appliqués.

Tulip flower base
Cut 8 from green check.

Vase lip
Cut 8 from red print.

Vase
Cut 8 from green check.

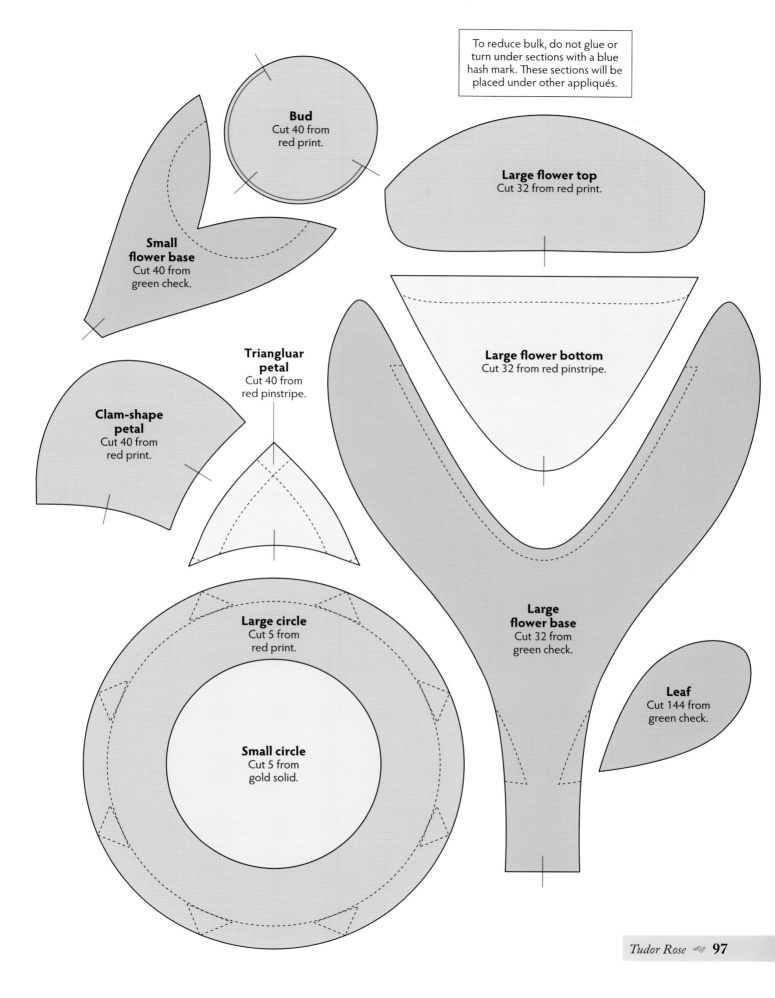

To reduce bulk, do not glue or turn under sections with a blue hash mark. These sections will be placed under other appliqués.

Bud
Cut 40 from red print.

Large flower top
Cut 32 from red print.

Small flower base
Cut 40 from green check.

Large flower bottom
Cut 32 from red pinstripe.

Triangluar petal
Cut 40 from red pinstripe.

Clam-shape petal
Cut 40 from red print.

Large flower base
Cut 32 from green check.

Large circle
Cut 5 from red print.

Small circle
Cut 5 from gold solid.

Leaf
Cut 144 from green check.

Sweet Mint

BY EDYTA SITAR

Beautiful rich reds and softer pinks combine with green to make a wall or lap quilt fit for any time of the year. If you have never tried curved piecing, this pattern is a good place to start—the curves are large and gentle, which will have you singing the praises of curved piecing in no time! ~Edyta

Materials

Yardage is based on 42"-wide fabric.

1 fat eighth *each* of 12 assorted red prints for blocks

1 fat eighth *each* of 12 assorted light prints for blocks

⅔ yard of green botanical print for block backgrounds

⅔ yard of cream solid for block backgrounds

⅝ yard of cream polka dot for border

⅝ yard of green print for block centers and binding

2¾ yards of fabric for backing

49" × 61" piece of batting

Template plastic

Freezer paper

Fabric glue

Cutting

All measurements include ¼" seam allowances. Make templates using patterns A and B on page 103.

From *each* of the assorted red prints, cut:
8 A pieces (96 total)

From *each* of the assorted light prints, cut:
8 A pieces (96 total)

From the green botanical print, cut:
24 B pieces

From the cream solid, cut:
24 B pieces

From the cream polka dot, cut:
5 strips, 3½" × 42"

From the green print, cut:
1 strip, 3" × 42", for circle appliqués
6 strips, 2½" × 42"

By Edyta Sitar

QUILT SIZE: 42½" × 54½"   **BLOCK SIZE:** 12" × 12"

Assembling the Blocks

Press all seam allowances as indicated by the arrows.

1. Select eight matching light A pieces and eight matching red A pieces for each block.

2. Alternating the red and light, sew together two light and two red A pieces to make a unit. Make four A units.

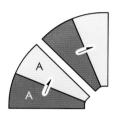

Make 4.

3. Mark the center of a green B piece by folding it in half and making a crease. With right sides together, align the crease with the center seam of an A unit and pin. Align each edge and pin. With the B piece on the bottom and the A unit on top, add pins between the center and edges.

> ### ❧ Adjust Stitch Length ❧
>
> Edyta slightly reduced the stitch length on her machine when sewing the A and B pieces together. A shorter stitch length allows you to navigate the curves more easily.

4. With the B piece on the bottom, carefully sew the pieces together, removing pins as you go. Make two units with green B pieces and two units with cream B

pieces. The units should measure 6½" square, including seam allowances.

Make 2 of each unit,
6½" × 6½".

5. Sew the four units together, alternating green and cream backgrounds, to complete the block. It should measure 12½" square, including seam allowances. Make 12 blocks.

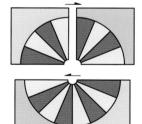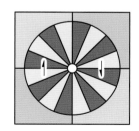

Make 12 units,
12½" × 12½".

6. Trace the circle pattern on page 103 onto freezer paper. Place this circle in the center of the blocks to ensure that all raw edges in the middle are covered. If it's too big or too small, adjust as needed. Once your paper template is exactly the size you need, cut 12 circles from freezer paper.

7. With fabric glue, adhere the dull side of the freezer paper circles to the wrong side of the green print, leaving at least ½" between each. Cut the circles ¼" larger than the freezer paper circle. Clip slightly into the seam allowances around the edges. Roll the fabric over the edge of the freezer paper and press to the shiny side. Prepare 12 circles.

Make 12 circles.

8. Center a circle on a block and adhere it with a few dots of fabric glue. Hand or machine appliqué the circle to the block. Remove the freezer paper and press the block gently from the wrong side. Repeat for each of the 12 blocks.

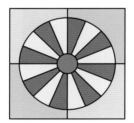

Make 12 blocks,
12½" × 12½".

❧ Machine Appliqué ❧

Use a size 90 needle, invisible nylon thread in the top of your machine, and cotton thread that matches the background fabric in the bobbin. Lower the top tension and use a close zigzag stitch, approximately 20 to 24 stitches to an inch. The width of the stitch should be narrow—just large enough that the stitches grab the background fabric and the edge of the appliqué. Stitch a sample using scrap fabrics to make sure your settings are where you want them.

Assembling the Quilt

1. Arrange the blocks in four rows of three blocks each, keeping the green background in the same position throughout. Sew the blocks into rows and then sew the rows together. The quilt center should measure 36½" × 48½".

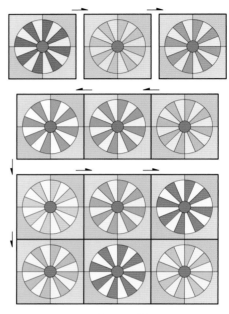

Quilt assembly

2. Sew the five polka dot 3½" × 42" strips together into one long length. Cut two strips, 48½" long, for the sides and two strips, 42½" long, for the top and bottom. Sew the longer borders to sides of the quilt center and then the shorter borders to the top and bottom. The quilt top should measure 42½" × 54½".

Finishing the Quilt

For more details on any finishing steps, visit ShopMartingale.com/HowtoQuilt for free downloadable information.

1. Layer the backing, batting, and quilt top; baste the layers together.

2. Quilt by hand or machine. The quilt shown is machine quilted with cookie-cutter shapes and meandering lines.

3. Use the green 2½"-wide strips to make binding, and then attach the binding to the quilt.

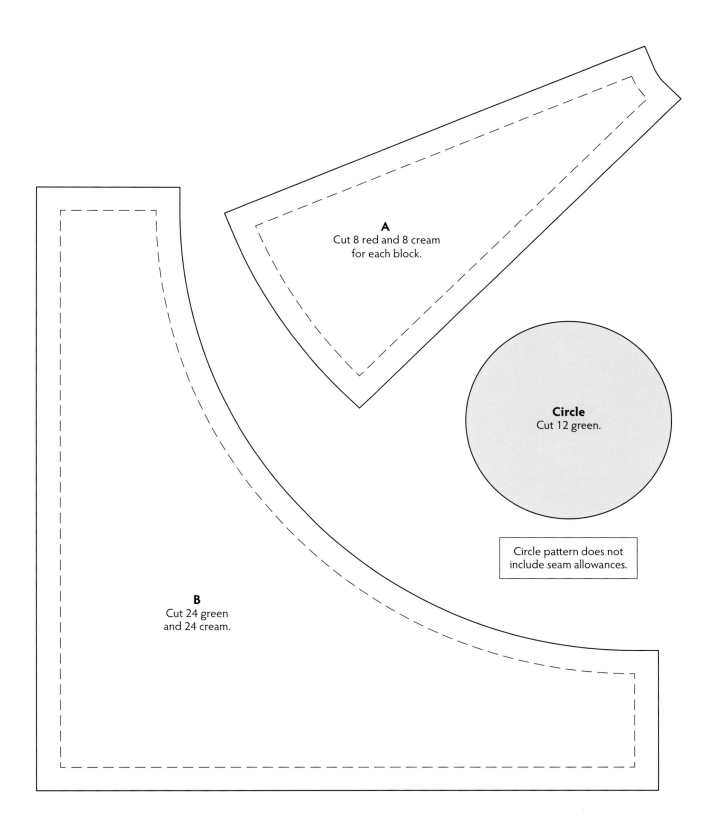

A
Cut 8 red and 8 cream
for each block.

Circle
Cut 12 green.

Circle pattern does not
include seam allowances.

B
Cut 24 green
and 24 cream.

CHRISTMAS STAR

BY PAULA BARNES AND MARY ELLEN ROBISON

Classic colors combined with a gorgeous Star block and double diagonal chain result in an extraordinary bed quilt. The piecing is easy and the quilt is truly more than the sum of its parts. Choose just three fabrics and you're good to go. ~Paula and Mary Ellen

Materials

Yardage is based on 42"-wide fabric.

3¼ yards of red print for blocks and middle border

7¾ yards of cream solid for blocks, borders, and binding

⅝ yard of green print for blocks

7¾ yards of fabric for backing

93" × 93" piece of batting

Cutting

All measurements include ¼" seam allowances.

From the red print, cut:

2 strips, 2½" × 42"

65 strips, 1½" × 42"; crosscut *29* of the strips into:
    96 rectangles, 1½" × 2½"
    576 squares, 1½" × 1½"

From the *lengthwise* grain of the cream solid, cut:

2 strips, 5½" × 84½"

2 strips, 5½" × 74½"

4 strips, 2½" × 86"; crosscut into 136 squares, 2½" × 2½"

2 strips, 1½" × 72½"

2 strips, 1½" × 70½"

From the remaining cream solid, cut on the *crosswise* grain:

13 strips, 3½" × 42"; crosscut into 100 rectangles, 3½" × 4½"

32 strips, 2½" × 42"; crosscut *22* of the strips into 344 squares, 2½" × 2½"

24 strips, 1½" × 42"

From the green print, cut:

2 strips, 2½" × 42"; crosscut into 24 squares, 2½" × 2½"

8 strips, 1½" × 42"; crosscut into 192 squares, 1½" × 1½"

Making the Double Nine Patch Blocks

Press all seam allowances as indicated by the arrows.

1. Aligning the long edges, sew together one cream and two red 1½" × 42" strips to make strip set A. Make eight. Cut the strip sets into 200 A segments, 1½" × 3½".

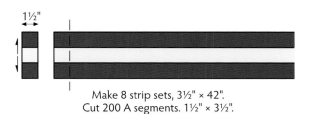

Make 8 strip sets, 3½" × 42".
Cut 200 A segments. 1½" × 3½".

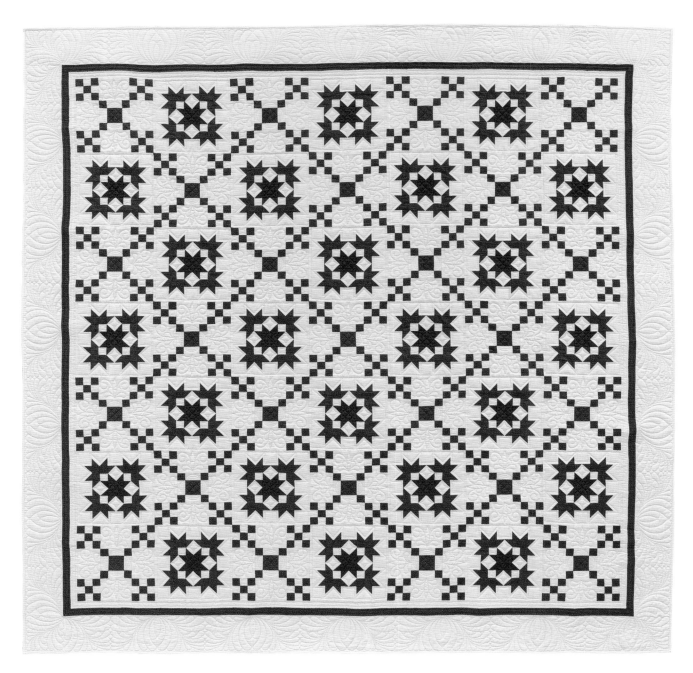

By Paula Barnes; pieced by Mary Ellen Robison; machine quilted by Marcella Pickett

QUILT SIZE: 84½" × 84½" ❧ **BLOCK SIZE:** 10" × 10"

2. In the same manner, join one red and two cream 1½" × 42" strips to make strip set B. Make four. Cut the strip sets into 100 B segments, 1½" × 3½".

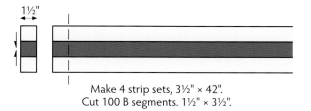

Make 4 strip sets, 3½" × 42".
Cut 100 B segments. 1½" × 3½".

3. Sew together two A segments and one B segment to make a nine-patch unit. Make 100 units that measure 3½" square, including seam allowances.

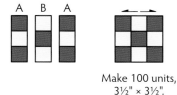

Make 100 units,
3½" × 3½".

4. Aligning the long edges, sew together two red 1½" × 42" strips and one cream 2½" × 42" strip to make strip set C. Make two. Cut the strip sets into 50 C segments, 1½" × 4½".

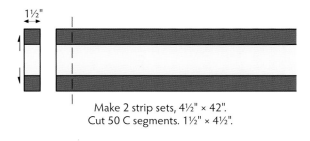

Make 2 strip sets, 4½" × 42".
Cut 50 C segments. 1½" × 4½".

5. In the same manner, join two cream 1½" × 42" strips and one red 2½" × 42" strip to make strip set D. Make two. Cut the strip sets into 25 D segments, 2½" × 4½".

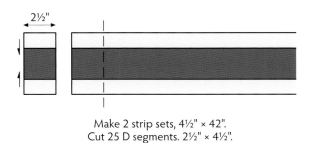

Make 2 strip sets, 4½" × 42".
Cut 25 D segments. 2½" × 4½".

6. Sew together two C segments and one D segment to make a center nine-patch unit. Make 25 center units that measure 4½" square, including seam allowances.

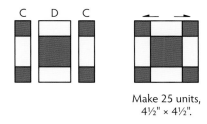

Make 25 units,
4½" × 4½".

7. Lay out four nine-patch units, four cream 3½" × 4½" rectangles, and one center unit in three rows. Sew the pieces together into rows. Join the rows to make a Double Nine Patch block. Make 25 blocks that measure 10½" square, including seam allowances.

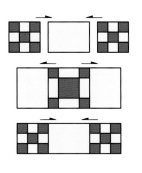

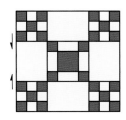

Make 25 blocks,
10½" × 10½".

Making the Star Blocks

1. Draw a diagonal line from corner to corner on the wrong side of each red and green 1½" square.

2. Align a marked red 1½" square, right side down, in one corner of a cream 2½" square as shown. Sew on the drawn line. Trim seam allowances to ¼". In the same manner, add a marked red 1½" square to the adjacent corner to make a unit. Make 192 units.

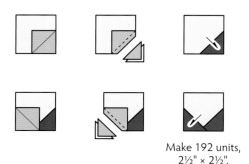

Make 192 units,
2½" × 2½".

3. Aligning the long edges, sew together one red and one cream 1½" × 42" strip to make strip set E. Make four. Cut the strip sets into 96 E segments, 1½" × 2½".

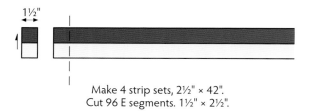

1½"

Make 4 strip sets, 2½" × 42".
Cut 96 E segments. 1½" × 2½".

4. Sew together one red 1½" × 2½" rectangle and one E segment to make a pieced square unit, 2½" × 2½", including seam allowances. Make 96.

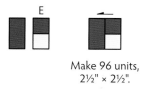

E

Make 96 units,
2½" × 2½".

5. Align marked red and green 1½" squares on opposite corners of a cream 2½" square, right sides together as shown. Sew on the drawn lines. Trim the seam allowances to ¼". In the same manner, add marked red and green 1½" squares to the remaining corners. Repeat to make 96 square-in-a-square units measuring 2½" square, including seam allowances.

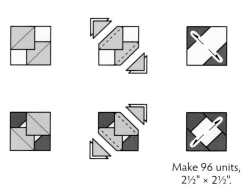

Make 96 units,
2½" × 2½".

6. Lay out eight cream 2½" squares, eight units from step 2, four units from step 4, four square-in-a-square units, and one green 2½" square in five rows as shown. Sew together the pieces in each row. Join the rows to make a block that measures 10½" square, including seam allowances. Make 24 blocks.

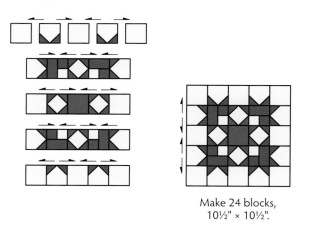

Make 24 blocks,
10½" × 10½".

Assembling the Quilt Top

1. Lay out the blocks in seven rows of seven blocks each, alternating blocks. Join the blocks in each row. Join the rows. The quilt center should be 70½" square, including seam allowances.

2. Referring to the adding borders illustration on page 110, sew the cream 1½" × 70½" strips to opposite edges of the quilt center. Sew the cream 1½" × 72½" strips to the remaining edges. The quilt top should now be 72½" square, including seam allowances.

3. Join the remaining red 1½" × 42" strips end to end and press the seam allowances open. Trim the pieced length into two 74½"-long middle-border strips and two 72½"-long middle-border strips. Sew

the shorter strips to opposite edges of the quilt center. Sew the longer strips to the remaining edges. The quilt top should now be 74½" square, including seam allowances.

❧ A Versatile Block ❧

Using a Double Nine Patch block as an alternate block (whether in a straight setting or on point) beautifully frames both pieced and appliquéd blocks, and also creates a charming double-chain effect.

Quilt assembly

4. Sew the cream 5½" × 74½" strips to opposite edges of the quilt top. Sew the cream 5½" × 84½" strips to the remaining edges to complete the quilt top. It should measure 84½" square.

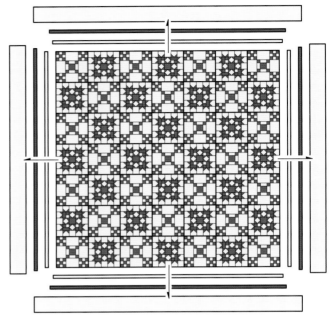

Adding the borders

Finishing the Quilt

For more details on any finishing steps, visit ShopMartingale.com/HowtoQuilt for free downloadable information.

1. Layer the backing, batting, and quilt top; baste the layers together.

2. Quilt by hand or machine. The quilt shown is machine quilted with a fleur-de-lis design in the Double Nine Patch blocks. The Star blocks are outline quilted. The squares in the block centers feature a diagonal grid. The borders are stitched in a lovely feather design.

3. Use the remaining cream 2½" × 42" strips to make binding, and then attach the binding to the quilt.

About the Contributors

Susan Ache

Having always loved handwork and embroidery, Susan designs and creates quilts using everyday life as her inspiration and fabric as her playground.

Lissa Alexander

Online she's ModaLissa, but by day, Lissa heads up the Moda marketing team. By night, she's quilting, blogging, designing, and more at ModaLissa.com. Her wish? "I hope you get time to sit and sew. It's good for the soul."

Paula Barnes and Mary Ellen Robison

Paula and Mary Ellen met more than 20 years ago and quickly formed a friendship that went beyond their love of quilting and reproduction fabric to become Red Crinoline Quilts. Paula also designs for Marcus Fabrics. Visit RedCrinolineQuilts.com.

Lisa Bongean

Lisa owns Primitive Gatherings Quilt Shop and is a designer for Moda Fabrics. She teaches and shares her designs across the country. You can find her at LisaBongean.com.

Pam Buda

Pam began publishing quilt patterns in 2004 under her company name, Heartspun Quilts. She creates reproduction fabrics for Marcus Fabrics, has designed quilts for national quilting magazines, and travels to teach at guilds, shops, shows, retreats, and on quilting cruises. Visit her at HeartspunQuilts.com.

Betsy Chutchian

Betsy is an author, a designer for Moda Fabrics, and the cofounder of the 19th-Century Patchwork Divas. Visit her at BetsysBestQuiltsandMore.blogspot.com.

Carol Hopkins

Through her pattern business, Carol Hopkins Designs, Carol markets quilt patterns that she has designed for eighteenth- and nineteenth-century reproduction fabrics. Visit her at CarolHopkinsDesigns.com.

Sheryl Johnson

Sheryl opened her quilt shop, Temecula Quilt Co., in 2007, featuring reproduction fabrics and traditional quilts with a vintage look. She hosts popular quilt-alongs on her blog for fans who aren't able to visit her brick-and-mortar shop in person. Sheryl is also a designer for Marcus Fabrics. Learn more at TemeculaQuiltCo.com.

Sandy Klop

Sandy creates her own designs under the name American Jane Patterns and is also a designer for Moda Fabrics. Visit AmericanJane.com.

Jo Morton

Jo's love of antique quilts has inspired her since the early 1980s. She loves to make small versions of vintage quilts to enjoy in her home and share with quilters. Follow Jo on Instagram @joquilts.

Laurie Simpson

Laurie is a lifelong needle artist whose quilts have been featured in a variety of publications. You can visit her online at MinickandSimpson.blogspot.com.

Edyta Sitar

The owner of Laundry Basket Quilts, Edyta loves creating quilts and designing fabrics for Andover Fabrics. Visit her online at LaundryBasketQuilts.com.

Karen Styles

Karen says, "The color red is my favorite color. And a little-known fact about me is that I only ever wear red shoes." Visit her at SomersetPatchwork.com.au.

Corey Yoder

A quilty mom of two girls and wife to one great husband, Corey enjoys playing with fabric in the form of quilts and quilt design. You can find her at CorianderQuilts.com.